LIVE WELL

15.10.10

HEALTH SCIENCES LIBRARY

SPH   B14325

NOTTS

Family
Experiences
of BIPOLAR
DISORDER

D0988186

by the same author

Surviving Post-Natal Depression
At Home, No One Hears You Scream
Cara Aiken
Forewords by Ian Brockington and Denise Welch
ISBN 978 1 85302 861 8

of related interest

Silent Grief
Living in the Wake of Suicide
Christopher Lukas and Henry M. Seiden
ISBN 978 1 84310 847 4

Survival Strategies for Parenting Children with Bipolar Disorder
Innovative Parenting and Counseling Techniques for Helping Children
with Bipolar Disorder and the Conditions That May Occur With It
George T. Lynn
ISBN 978 1 85302 921 9

Alphabet Kids – From ADD to Zellweger Syndrome
A Guide to Developmental, Neurobiological and Psychological
Disorders for Parents and Professionals
Robbie Woliver
ISBN 978 1 84310 880 1

The Pits and the Pendulum
A Life with Bipolar Disorder
Brian Adams
ISBN 978 1 84310 104 8

Family Experiences

of BIPOLAR

DISORDER

The ups, the downs and the bits in between

CARA AIKEN

FOREWORD BY PROFESSOR ANNE FARMER

WM 207
AIICEN

Jessica Kingsley Publishers
London and Philadelphia

First published in 2010
by Jessica Kingsley Publishers
116 Pentonville Road
London N1 9JB, UK
and
400 Market Street, Suite 400
Philadelphia, PA 19106, USA

www.jkp.com

Copyright © Cara Aiken 2010
Foreword copyright © Anne Farmer 2010

All rights reserved. No part of this publication may be reproduced in any material form
(including photocopying or storing it in any medium by electronic means and whether or
not transiently or incidentally to some other use of this publication) without the written
permission of the copyright owner except in accordance with the provisions of the
Copyright, Designs and Patents Act 1988 or under the terms of a licence issued by the
Copyright Licensing Agency Ltd, Saffron House, 6–10 Kirby Street, London EC1N 8TS.
Applications for the copyright owner's written permission to reproduce any part of this
publication should be addressed to the publisher.
Warning: The doing of an unauthorised act in relation to a copyright work may result in
both a civil claim for damages and criminal prosecution.

Library of Congress Cataloging in Publication Data
Aiken, Cara, 1964-
  Family experiences of bipolar disorder / Cara Aiken.
      p. cm.
  Includes bibliographical references.
  ISBN 978-1-84310-935-8 (alk. paper)
  1. Aiken, Cara, 1964---Health. 2. Manic-depressive persons--Family relationships. 3.
Manic-depressive illness. I. Title.
  RC516.A368 2010
  362.196'895--dc22
                                        2009050425

British Library Cataloguing in Publication Data
A CIP catalogue record for this book is available from the British Library

ISBN 978 1 84310 935 8

Printed and bound in the United States by
Thomson-Shore, 7300 Joy Road, Dexter, MI 48130

To my darling children, Georgina and Tasha.

You have been my inspiration for writing this book. You have grown into the most beautiful girls, inside and out. I appreciate every moment I spend with you and I love you both with all my heart and soul.

Mummy

Contents

Acknowledgements

I have so many people I wish to mention, and 'thank you' just doesn't feel a powerful enough phrase. But here I go...

First, I have to mention my very good friend Tessa whom I regard as my mentor. I turned to her some months back, when I hit a point where I had lost all confidence in my writing. I was struggling mentally with particularly low self-esteem. I had reached crisis point, totally lost all inspiration, and was fighting against my decision to give up on the book. She stepped in immediately (Tessa does come across as a rather authoritative person) and there was basically no choice in the matter – I *had* to continue, there was no way she would allow me to drop out at this stage. Tessa is the reason this book is now complete. She has given me endless encouragement and support; she's proof read, edited, advised, and praised me constantly on my writing. She's such a strict 'teacher'! She laid down some rules, gently nagged me if I slacked, and 'held my hand' to the very end. I thank you so much, Tessa, I wouldn't have made it without you and I genuinely feel honoured to have you as my friend.

This book would not have been possible without all my contributors – Tara, Sandy, Sharon, Tracey, Jo, Phaedra, Michael, Paul, Karen, Koulla, Michel, Debbie and Kate – as well as the stories from anonymous contributors. You have been fantastic, thank you all so very much and I apologize for driving you all mad at times! I thank all the children for their contributions – Hannah, Jack, David, James, Bethan, Georgina and Tasha. You have all been very brave for writing something for this book. I would also like to say how grateful I am to the family members who kindly wrote something for Chapter 5, 'Adult Relationships and Bipolar Disorder' – Basil, Lauren, Mum, Dad, Jody, Rob, Sue, David, Heather and Claire.

I very much appreciate the generous contributions from Professor Quentin Spender, Professor Nicholas Craddock and Dr Ian Jones. Once again, huge thanks to you all.

I would like to thank MDF The Bipolar Organization for all your help with my research appeal.

Thank you to my wonderful family who have stuck by me through thick and thin. Some would say you can't choose your family but you can choose your friends. I'd choose all of you every time. I love you.

I would like to mention some of my very good friends for their friendship, support and encouragement. Thank you, Tracey, for keeping my flame alight – you've been more than a great encouragement for me. I am truly grateful that this book has created such a wonderful friendship between us. Sandy, my bezzy, we've held each other up for almost ten years. Thank you for sharing all our ups and downs, our hopes and our dreams of eventual success. Well done for finally completing *your* book. I knew you could do it! I cannot let my lifelong friend Karen slip by without a mention – you've been an amazing doctor, psychiatrist, counsellor and health advisor – you are truly talented and I thank you so much for everything.

To all of my other friends – those of you who have remained by my side despite my erratic behaviour, unreliability, tears, good times and bad – I love you all – you have been fantastic.

Stephen Jones (Jessica Kingsley Publishers) – thank you for being so patient and for having continued faith in me.

Finally, and most importantly, I'd like to mention Basil, Gina and Tasha. Basil, darling, I really cannot find any words that are strong enough to express my gratitude to you for your undying and endless love, towards me and the girls. You have been the family support beam in our home. You have stood by me and the girls through so many difficult periods. You have so much love and warmth in your heart, I admire your strengths and I will never fail to recognize that you have a beautiful soul. You've made me so very happy. I adore you more than words can say.

I want to thank my darling daughters, Georgina and Tasha, for inspiring me to write this book. You have both been so devoted to me despite my tears, embarrassing and extremely childish behaviour and the two or three times I've ever 'really' shouted and made you scared! I will *never* let you down, girls, you are my life, my reason to fight – I will always be here to 'tuck you in' each night, I will love you unconditionally, forever and ever and ever. Thank you for always making me laugh, and for making me so proud that you are mine. Basil, Gina and Tasha, you are my world.

Foreword

It can be argued that bipolar disorder has been the "forgotten" major mental disorder in recent decades, since public funding and treatment initiatives have been mainly directed into improving the experiences of those suffering from other major mental disorders. Recently however, the often debilitating nature of the illness has been highlighted by the courage of high profile sufferers: well-known public figures who have 'come out' about their own illnesses.

In this book, Cara Aiken writes about her own illness and uses these experiences and those of other sufferers to discuss all aspects of living with bipolar disorder. She takes a 360 degree view of the disorder, starting from the point of view of the person suffering from it and describing the various phases and types of bipolar disorder – manic and depressive episodes as well as rapid cycling and mixed states. She then goes on to present the impact of bipolar disorder on family, friends, colleagues and children. The professional view is represented with readily understood yet informed contributions by international experts. All aspects of bipolar disorder are covered, from its onset through to its long-term management in old age. The contentious issues of childhood onset bipolar disorder are addressed, as are the complications of bipolar disorder occurring in the immediate aftermath of childbirth.

Written with a light touch, Cara has succeeded in informing and reassuring as well as entertaining and as we close the book after reaching the end we know that we have learned a great deal as well as acquired a much greater empathy for those with this somewhat neglected illness.

Professor Anne Farmer
Institute of Psychiatry

Preface

There is a lot of material written about bipolar disorder from the perpective of the person with the condition. This book also aims to provide this perspective, but in addition it aims to provide information about the disorder and to show its effect on the family as well as the person living with it. The book contains accounts from myself alongside accounts from other sufferers, to depict in real terms life within a family where bipolar disorder exists.

As the author of this book, I hope to act as a guide through the contributions and perspectives gathered together within it, and I aim to write with total honesty throughout, in lay terms, to provide you with as simple as possible an insight into a confusing and life-changing disorder.

I write from a position of personal experience of bipolar disorder. I strongly believe that I was born a very 'sensitive soul'. I am always 'too' empathic to an extent where I 'feel' another's pain – literally – it pervades my heart, my mind, my being.

I love too hard – cry too hard, laugh too hard – I never 'hate'. I don't do useless emotions – I live with them each and every day. Happy, sad, happy, sad…

I feel another's happiness as if it were my own – I indulge myself in it. I rejoice in it… When I am happy, the stars begin to look brighter, the grass is a vivid shade of green, the clouds are cotton wool in the sky on which angels sing. My mind is crystal clear, my blood is liquid gold, my mind alert, my words eloquent, ideas flow, goals are achievable. I feel young again. My heart sings and dances. I'm fortunate, lucky, happy, loved, admired… I'm a celebrity, I'm famous…

But sometimes, just sometimes – I feel my 'angel of death' following me through every stage of each episode – tapping my shoulder, beckoning me to join her.

In this book, I combine my own personal experience of life with bipolar disorder and those of others with useful information written by psychologists. Each chapter is designed to address different aspects of this disorder, and gives a 'voice' to the family members and the children who were keen to discuss the impact it has had on *their* lives.

I was inspired to write this book because of seeing the effects my illness has had on my own two daughters, Georgina and Tasha, my partner Basil, and the family as a whole, and the challenges it can present. I hope that it will offer the many other families in a similar situation (and perhaps the professionals who work with them) some useful advice drawn from mine and the other contributors' stories, as well as giving hope that there really is life after a bipolar diagnosis, and some comfort in the knowledge that they are not alone.

Note: All contributors' stories are listed in the Appendix by family group for ease of reference.

Some contributors' names have been changed to protect their identity.

1

CHAPTER

Introducing
Bipolar Disorder

In this chapter, I first provide a general summary of common features of bipolar disorder, and incorporate within the explanations illustrations of what these features look like in reality for the person living with bipolar disorder.

About bipolar disorder

Bipolar disorder, also known as manic depression, is a brain disorder that causes unusual and extreme shifts in a person's mood. It can affect their energy levels and ability to function. Most people have normal ups and downs, but for someone with bipolar disorder, the mood shifts are severe.

It is not yet fully understood what causes bipolar disorder. The condition can run in families, although this is not always the case. It typically develops between the ages of 18 and 24, but it can occur at any age. The disorder is a relatively common condition, with around 1 person in 100 currently being diagnosed.

Many people suffer for years before they are given a diagnosis and treatment. Typically, the depressive phase comes first. In many cases, this can last, on and off, for years. A manic phase can develop some time later, after which the diagnosis of depression may change to bipolar disorder.

Bipolar disorder is a long-term illness that must be carefully managed throughout a person's life.

It can take a period of time after the initial diagnosis to learn how best to cope with the ups and downs. Various medications may be tried until the right one that works for the individual is found.

Symptoms of bipolar disorder

Symptoms of bipolar disorder can cause dramatic mood swings from overly high to feelings of sadness and hopelessness. Severe changes in energy and behaviour go along with these changes in mood.

The periods of highs and lows are called episodes of mania and depression. Other symptoms can manifest alongside the mania and depression, for example hypomania, psychosis and mixed state episodes. In some cases, the sufferer can also experience rapid cycling where the mood changes swing back and forth more frequently.

Below are descriptions of symptoms for the following types of episode or condition, with an illustration for each:

- depressive episode
- hypomanic episode
- manic episode
- psychosis episode
- mixed state episode
- rapid cycling.

Symptoms of a depressive episode

- lasting sad, anxious, or empty mood
- loss of energy
- prolonged sadness
- decreased activity and energy
- restlessness and irritability
- inability to concentrate or make decisions
- increased feelings of worry and anxiety

- less interest and enjoyment of everyday activities
- feelings of guilt and hopelessness
- feelings of worthlessness
- thoughts of suicide
- change in appetite (either eating more or eating less)
- change in sleep patterns (either sleeping more or sleeping less)
- feelings of guilt and despair
- feeling pessimistic about everything.

Depressive episode example: anonymous

My mood has crashed as low as it could possibly go. I am struggling to get through each and every hour. I think I'm getting on everyone's nerves but can't help reaching out to all my friends for support today. I just keep ringing everyone and crying.

I feel as though I have reached breaking point. There's always a trigger to my depression. Yesterday I saw my mum cry, and that was the final straw.

After she left, I spiralled into despair. I always try so hard to hide my episodes from the children, but today they saw me crying hysterically. I am ashamed and guilty that I could not control myself until the girls were in bed and asleep. But the tears were coming out and I broke down in front of them. The depressive episodes are destroying me. My bed is my only safety, and offers me a brief escape from the harsh reality of my illness. Today, all I have wanted to do is sleep. I don't know how much longer I can live with this mess of a life.

Symptoms of a hypomanic episode

- similar symptoms to a manic episode (see below), but less severe
- increased energy

- euphoric mood
- high self-esteem
- good functioning levels
- enhanced productivity
- irritability
- denial that anything is wrong to friends and family.

Hypomanic expisode example: anonymous

> Rapid thoughts transferred from mind to paper – almost too rapid at times to capture in a sentence. It feels good to be working again. I feel proud of today's achievements. I have regained my self-worth. I almost forget the past few months where I haven't remotely had the ability to write – the months of numbness, the period of time where my mind has been blank. All the bad times seem worth it when I am feeling so well. I'm productive, energized and catching up on neglected tasks. Have moved all the furniture around in the house – it feels like a new start. Having so much fun with the kids. Been shopping today and bought everything in sight! I have great ideas for a business plan, it's totally 'fool proof', I'm the happiest I have been for so long, so happy it's fantastic. Everyone around me seems so much happier too.
>
> Back in contact with all the friends I have been avoiding while I was ill. The ability to captivate people once again with my 'bubble'. Oh God, please let this last.

Symptoms of a manic episode

- feeling extremely happy, elated or euphoric
- increased physical and mental activity and energy
- racing thoughts
- increased talking, more rapid speech than normal
- ambitious, often grandiose plans
- risk taking

- impulsive activity such as spending sprees, sexual indiscretion
- decreased sleep without experiencing fatigue
- distracted, can't concentrate well
- a lasting period of behaviour that is different from usual
- abuse of drugs, particularly cocaine, alcohol and sleeping medications
- provocative, intrusive, or aggressive behaviour
- not eating
- denial that anything is wrong.

Manic episode example: anonymous

I am aware that I'm feeling on the higher end of the scale, but *I am not* experiencing a manic episode. What is all the fuss about? Can I not just enjoy the productivity and creative ideas which encompass me at this time? Why is everyone pouncing on me insisting I take extra medication? I feel well. I feel happy. I am high functioning. I am enjoying myself. This is a great opportunity to catch up on neglected chores, neglected work, neglected writing. But it doesn't stop... The feeling of productivity shifts into making grandiose plans. The creativity develops into an impossible mission; the happiness becomes elation, the high functioning turns into agitation, the enjoyment results in despair. I should have taken the medication my family insisted upon me taking. That's what all the fuss was about.

Symptoms of a psychosis episode

Severe episodes of mania or depression can include the symptoms of psychosis:

- sensing the presence of things that are not actually there
- hallucinations

- delusions of strongly held beliefs – unusual or cultural concepts, e.g. 'Jesus said...to me', or 'God told me', or 'I believed my child was the son of Jesus'
- confused and disturbed thoughts
- a lack of insight and self-awareness.

Psychosis episode example: Tara

In April 2007 my dog, Poppy, died, she had been very poorly for a few weeks, and I had to make the difficult decision to bring her life to an end.

This was a stressor which I feel greatly contributed to my condition. My consultant had also decided to reduce my medications. During this time I entered into a period of psychosis, with hallucinations, auditory and visual, and delusions.

There was a telepathic lady living in the television. Telepathically, she taught me to always face my fears and to say, 'It's OK, it'll be all right, I trust you,' in situations I feared. She told me that I always had to obey her commands. I thought that she worked for some secret organization helping people and telepathically I was assessed by her for an assignment to work on the streets in the inner city of a city I didn't know. She communicated to me that I was to be picked up and dropped off without anything except the clothes I had on me. I had to leave everything in my life behind, including my cats. I was commanded by her to write a suicide note to my mum to leave behind, which I did so that they (anyone) wouldn't come looking for me. I was to be drugged with heroin and alcohol and taken during the night to a city and was to live as a drug addict and alcoholic on the streets and work with the people I met. I was to live like them with nothing, and to have no further contact with my old life in Leeds.

On another occasion, I phoned my sister on her mobile and got my brother-in-law Duncan instead. In the background I heard children screaming and screaming, and I could hear a hammer banging. I shouted at him 'I know what you're doing.' I told him I could hear the children screaming. He said he was at work and that if he had been at home, that would have been OK. I believed he was at home torturing the children. Then I phoned the police and told them what I had heard.

I was admitted to hospital on a section[1] as being in a state of mania. I was unable to communicate as my expressions were described as a 'word salad'. When I tried to think, I could only think of three phrases: 'Willy Wonka', 'up the garden path' and 'round the corner', which I replied to most questions asked of me.

When I arrived at the Becklin Hospital, I was still in the mode of having to face my fears. I was seeing doors closing on their own with no one around. I saw door handles moving up and down when no one was around them. Lights went off.

On a number of occasions, I believed that I had grown a penis. I believed that I could feel it through my trousers and I would go to my room to check. I was so convinced of this, that I sat planning how I was going to cope when they moved me in with the men. I believed that it was God's will.

The biggest thing that happened for me while in hospital was my experiences with God. I had been a non-believer in God for 26 years. From the moment I arrived, God's presence was in my room. I put various things I had heard or seen down to God. I also had a £30 bottle of perfume and £60 and some clothes go missing. I thought that God wanted me to live without them. Because I thought I wasn't supposed to have any luxuries, I took off my £400 watch and threw it in the bin.

I didn't know where I was and believed that I was in heaven or somewhere between life and death, and that I must have either tried to kill myself, or been killed and was waiting to enter heaven. I thought that everyone there was an angel.

1 The Mental Health Act (1983) is divided into sections. In the UK when someone is admitted to hospital under compulsion this is commonly known as 'being sectioned'.

In the faith room, we sang 'in God's house for evermore my dwelling place shall be', and then I believed that I would be with God forever. I thought that God had saved me from the terrors of home and I prayed at every opportunity I got.

I met Linda (another patient in the hospital) and thought that she was a senior angel. When I saw my mum and other people, I thought that they were all really Linda in different forms, testing me for heaven. Sometimes things appeared in my room, like shampoo, and I thought that these were a gift from God.

I wrote a prayer.

Whilst eating a chocolate, half of my front tooth crumbled and broke off. I thought that this was because I was to live minimally and not eat chocolate ever again. I believed that this was a miracle from God, and went round smiling about it.

Symptoms of a mixed state episode

A mixed state episode is a period where a manic and a depressive episode are present at the same time (all these symptoms can happen in a mixed state episode within a course of minutes).

- either an elated, happy mood or an irritable, angry, unpleasant mood
- hopelessness, irritability
- uncontrollable swings of racing thoughts which coincide with feelings of despair and blackness
- feeling highly activated but also full of anguish and despair
- pressured and rapid speech which can co-exist with impulsive, out-of-control thoughts of self-destruction.

Mixed state episode example: anonymous

My day started with a mixed state episode, which I attempted to treat with Valium. Feeling manic but agitated. My energies are high but I feel incredibly irritable. I don't want anyone to talk to me, everything is annoying. Everyone is annoying. I have no concentration and the children keep asking me questions which I cannot answer. I can barely listen. All I want to do is sleep to escape these feelings, but my mind is racing. It's 7pm and I have a glass of brandy to calm me down. I have another glass and feel some relief from the agitation. I don't like to drink as it can make me depressed.

But tonight I need alcohol and continue to drink. The result of my day was a drunken stupor and finally passing out. My boyfriend carried me up to bed.

Rapid cycling

Rapid cycling is defined as four or more manic, hypomanic or depressive episodes in any 12-month period. With rapid cycling, mood swings shift from low to high and back again, and can occur over periods of a few days and sometimes even hours.

There are various forms of rapid cycling. 'Ultradian cycling' is defined as when several mood changes occur within a day or even an hour.

Rapid cycling example: anonymous

I can't seem to get a hold of this rapid cycling even with my new medications. I'm emotionally and physically exhausted. I'm finding it impossible to wake up in the morning and then, when I do, I'm on the go all day like a crazed woman. A couple of days later I can't move. I'm depressed, in bed, crying and cannot face the world. My doctor has confirmed that this is a severe form of rapid cycling. I'm trying new medications constantly but nothing seems to work. It is becoming impossible not knowing what to expect each day. There is little if any stability right now. I wish someone could help me before I reach a point where I can no longer cope.

I hope that the above has provided you with an initial idea of what life is actually like behind the diagnosis of bipolar disorder. An important consideration that anyone with a diagnosis needs to know is how best to manage their condition.

The material that follows was kindly provided by Professor Nick Craddock MA, MB, ChB, MMedSci, PhD, FRCPsych, Consultant

Psychiatrist and Head of the Cardiff University Psychiatry Service, who is also Scientific Advisor to MDF The Bipolar Organization and Lead Researcher of the Bipolar Disorder Research Network (www.bdrn.org).

Managing bipolar disorder
Professor Nick Craddock

This short section provides some comments and suggestions about the management of bipolar disorder. A wide range of treatments are used for bipolar disorder and there are changes over time. An individual may be advised to change their medication according to their symptoms, and patients are sometimes offered alternative treatment options as new research is done. What follows is general information and guidance. For specific information on individual treatments (medications, talking treatments or other treatments) it is important to talk in detail with the mental health professionals who suggest the treatment, to ask for written information – and to ask questions! It is important to be an informed and active partner in treatment.

Be realistic and accept that bipolar disorder is a lifelong illness

Once a person has experienced a first episode of bipolar disorder, he or she is susceptible to other episodes of mood disorder (depression, mania or mixed state episodes) throughout life. However, when first diagnosed, a person often starts by thinking they are different from everyone else with bipolar disorder and believing that they will never have another episode. Unfortunately, this can make it take much longer for the person to get the best treatment.

Bipolar disorder varies greatly from person to person

The number and severity of episodes and overall pattern of illness varies enormously between individuals. Sometimes episodes seem to have a clear trigger. Sometimes they seem to come 'out of the blue'. Some people experience substantial anxiety and panic attacks; others do not. Often people develop delusions or hallucinations during severe episodes but many people with bipolar disorder never have such experiences. We do not yet understand why there is such an enormous range of experiences of bipolar illness. It can be expected that when research uncovers the explanations, psychiatrists will be much better able to tailor the most effective treatments to the person's illness.

Many treatments are used for bipolar disorder

Perhaps not surprisingly with such a wide range of ways bipolar disorder can affect someone, many different treatments can be used – some for specific types of symptom or episode (for example antidepressants or cognitive behaviour therapy for depression; lithium, some antiepileptics or antipsychotics for mania), and some to try to maintain mood stability (for example lithium, some antiepileptics and some antipsychotics). There are other treatments that help with symptoms such as anxiety and panic. None of these treatments works in every person. All treatments can have adverse effects and these are different in different people. It often takes some time (sometimes many months, or longer) to find the best treatments for a particular person with bipolar illness. Often this may involve a combination of different treatments. This process of finding the best treatments involves using the available evidence from research studies that have been done for the different treatments – together with careful trial and error of treatments.

Bipolar disorder treatment: the good news

The aim is always to find the treatment that is best for the individual – the optimal combination of beneficial effects on mood, whilst minimizing unwanted adverse effects. The good news is that with bipolar disorder (even the most severe forms) most individuals can achieve stabilization of their mood swings and related symptoms with the best treatment. Also, if a manic or depressive episode does occur, there are treatments available that are usually effective for the episode.

The importance of regular, long-term treatment in a partnership

Because bipolar disorder is a recurrent illness, long-term preventive treatment is usually important. The idea is to maintain a stable mood and prevent extreme swings into mania or depression (or mixed state episodes). In most cases it is best to follow a strategy that combines medication and so-called 'psychosocial' or 'psychoeducation' approaches. The latter involves the person with bipolar disorder learning about their illness and being pro-active in its management: for example, knowing how to recognize early signs of illness, knowing how to avoid precipitants of illness, using particular thinking strategies to deal with stress and anxiety – and, crucially, recognizing the importance of working in a productive partnership with the mental health professionals.

Finding out more

If you are reading this book, you are already learning about many aspects of the illness. It is a good idea to join an organization like MDF The Bipolar Organization (www.mdf.org.uk) and attend self-help groups; MDF also publishes a regular journal, *Pendulum*. There are educational courses and programmes available through some mental health services as well as MDF and it is well worth considering attending one. There are also equivalent organizations in most countries, such as The Depression and Bipolar Support Alliance in the USA.

Further, it is important to ask the mental health professionals as much as you want to know about your treatment. Discuss it in detail, read leaflets about the treatments you are being offered (available from your local services or from the Royal College of Psychiatrists (www.rcpsych.ac.uk) or MDF, and share ownership in the decision-making about treatments.

What can I do to help with maintaining mood stability?

Bipolar disorder is much better controlled with treatment that is taken regularly and in the prescribed dose. Many scientific studies have shown that one of the most important things that someone with bipolar disorder can do to avoid episodes of illness is to take prescribed medication regularly! There are also several important lifestyle choices that can be made that will help with mood stability. These include:

- Following a regular daily pattern, particularly regarding bed-time and sleep. (In many people with bipolar disorder, enforced sleep loss can trigger an episode – sleep loss may be due to things like night shifts, staying up all night to revise for exams or at a party, or jet lag.)

- Avoiding illicit or 'recreational' drugs. (Many drugs, including cannabis and cocaine, can trigger mood swings or psychotic episodes.)

- Avoiding excessive or binge drinking of alcohol. (Alcohol abuse is very common in people with bipolar disorder and makes mood swings much more difficult to control.)

- Avoiding excessive amounts of caffeine. (This can trigger mood swings.)

- Avoiding excessive life stresses. (Of course life is inherently stressful, but try to avoid setting up situations of excessive stress.)

Recognizing early signs of illness

Sometimes, even with regular treatment, an episode of illness may occur. The earlier such an episode is recognized, the more promptly and effectively it can be treated and it may be possible to 'nip it in the bud' and prevent a severe episode occurring. Thus, it is important to be able to recognize early signs of illness and to discuss any signs of illness with the mental health team as soon as possible. There are educational courses available through MDF and some health services that will help a person to recognize his or her 'relapse signature' of early signs of an episode.

Looking to the future

Whilst very helpful, current treatments are far from ideal. No treatment works in everyone with bipolar disorder and all treatments can have adverse effects in some people. We cannot yet predict with confidence who will experience positive or negative effects with each treatment so it can take a substantial amount of time to get a person on the best treatment. The main reasons for this are that we do not have a good scientific understanding of the causes and triggers of the illness. However, there are currently powerful research studies under way that will provide the new scientific understanding that, over the course of the next 10–20 years will have an enormous impact on the treatment and management of bipolar disorder. The experience of illness for the next generation of people with bipolar illness is likely to be very different. We can look forward to rapid, accurate diagnosis and more effective treatments, with fewer adverse effects, that can be tailored to the individual. We can be extremely optimistic about the future. However, to make this a reality will require a commitment of those with illness to help with, and be advocates for, research, together with a major concerted effort by researchers and, of course, a willingness of the government and research charities to fund the necessary research.

Those wishing to find out more about research in bipolar disorder can read regular articles in *Pendulum* (the journal of MDF The Bipolar Organization), look at the website of the Bipolar Disorder Research Network (www.bdrn.org) or, if you are based outside the UK, join a comparable organization closer to home.

As mentioned in the preface, this is a book about bipolar disorder and the family, as it is a condition that affects not only the person who is diagnosed, but also their friends, families and loved ones. An emotive issue that can cause anxiety to people living with bipolar disorder before they even have children is the impact of the diagnosis on childbirth – the fact that it can affect their own health, and also potentially their children.

In the section that follows, Dr Ian Jones BSc, MB, BS, PhD, MRCPsych who is Senior Lecturer and Consultant in Perinatal

Psychiatry at the Department of Psychological Medicine, Cardiff University, writes about this sensitive subject and outlines the facts.

Bipolar disorder and childbirth
Dr Ian Jones

Having a baby is a major event in the life of any woman. For those with bipolar disorder, a number of additional issues may arise.

Women with bipolar disorder may become unwell during pregnancy, but are at a particularly high risk of becoming ill following childbirth. Both manic and depressive episodes can occur at this time, and are often severe, and of the type that may be labelled 'puerperal psychosis' (or 'postpartum psychosis' – the term used in the USA).

Mood disturbance – elation, irritability and depression – is common, and as the name suggests, psychotic symptoms such as delusions and hallucinations often occur. Admission to hospital is usually required, but women often do very well with treatment – although many will have other episodes of illness, both related and unrelated to childbirth.

A number of studies have shown that episodes of puerperal psychosis occur following 25–50 per cent of deliveries born to bipolar women – that is up to 500 times more commonly than for women generally. Two groups of bipolar women are at even higher risk – those who have had a previous severe episode of illness following childbirth, and those with a relative who has suffered a severe postpartum episode. Of those women around 60 per cent or more may have an episode of puerperal psychosis.

Women who have had episodes of bipolar disorder must therefore take this risk very seriously. Even if you are currently very well, there is a real chance of becoming ill again shortly after the baby is born.

It is very important for women to recognize that this is a high risk time, and to let all those involved with your pregnancy know that you have had episodes of bipolar disorder, and that there is a real risk of becoming unwell again following delivery.

Your midwife, doctor (GP), health visitor and obstetrician should all be made aware of your past history of bipolar disorder. Your community psychiatric nurse, psychiatrist or other member of the mental health team need to be told about your pregnancy. Ideally, let your psychiatrist and doctor know that you want to get pregnant before you start trying for a baby. This will give them the chance to discuss any medications you are taking and what can be done to ensure you are as well as possible before becoming pregnant. Not all pregnancies are planned and if this is the situation you find yourself in, let people know as soon as possible.

In an ideal world, no woman would take any medication during pregnancy. No medications can be given a 100 per cent guarantee of safety. There are some medications, however, which a large number of women, around the world, have taken in pregnancy or when breast feeding, and no evidence of serious problems for the woman or her baby has come to light.

For some women it may be appropriate to take medication starting in late pregnancy or on the day of delivery to reduce the risk of becoming ill.

In some circumstances, it may still be appropriate that the medication is taken. The benefits from taking the medication may greatly outweigh any potential risks. The decision to take any particular medication is a complicated balance of the risks and benefits and will be different for each individual woman. Your doctor can discuss the risks and benefits with you, and we would encourage you to discuss this issue as early as possible.

Despite the potential problems discussed in this material, it is not intended to give the impression that women with bipolar disorder should avoid having children. Around the world, continuous research and clinical work (including through MDF The Bipolar Organization in the UK) helps women in this situation, and many bipolar women with children of all ages are very glad that they have had a family. There is good evidence that the majority of bipolar women thinking of starting a family, when presented with all the relevant information, make the decision to try for a baby.

2

Living with Bipolar Disorder

This chapter is devoted to the personal experiences of a variety of sufferers, providing a broader-ranging perspective of what it is like to live with bipolar disorder. It is important to comprehend fully what a person with bipolar disorder is going through, before discussing the impact this illness has on the family.

This book has been written to show how everyday life is for the sufferer, parents, siblings and children, in order to offer some support and encouragement to everyone involved, in a family where bipolar disorder exists. I have cut no corners: all personal experiences contained in this book have been written from the heart and with total honesty. It is important to mention at this point that neither I, nor any of those contributing their personal accounts to this chapter, are an authority on this illness. We are each just your average lay person who lives with an illness, but we do all share the experience of being in a position to speak with authority about our own lives and experiences, and we also share the challenge of somehow dealing with the complexity of everyday life.

First, let me tell you a little more about myself.

Living with bipolar disorder: Cara

Having lived with my bipolar since 1998, I have a clear insight – first into the illness, and second and more positively, into my own experience. Bipolar itself is so complex; my life since 1998 has become extremely complicated.

I embarked on this book with the confidence that I could describe my own personal account of living with bipolar disorder, with ease and accuracy. As I began to write up my story, it became apparent to me that this was not the case. I have spent endless hours, days, weeks and months struggling to unravel the memories. To salvage an accurate account has been almost impossible, due to severe memory loss, which I believe has been caused by so much medication. Today, as I write, I am fighting my memory loss, which I can only liken to putting together the pieces of an extremely difficult jigsaw puzzle. But here goes…

Prior to my breakdown in 1998, from about the age of 16, I lived in a perpetual state of 'hypomania', but this was not apparent to me. I loved the energy and speed, enjoyed life to the full, and was always the life and soul of every gathering. If something needed doing, I was the person who everyone turned to. I took it all in my stride; this was 'Cara', someone who people admired for my creativity and life skills. I searched out, and took on board, all the waifs and strays, feeling as though I could conquer the world.

Fresh out of school at 16, I worked in the television and radio department of a top and prestigious advertising agency. It was the perfect job for me – energetic, fast moving, with long hours, hard work, and hard play. The industry was vibrant and colourful, which fulfilled my passion for life. I was extremely successful in a short space of time, and almost made it to becoming a producer myself at just 18 years old.

This job was ultimately taken away from me by my boss, who was an unpleasant character and decided to employ another producer, even though the creative director, who also owned the agency, had previously insisted that the job was passed on to me. I was understandably bitterly disappointed by this and over-reacted while in an extremely hypomanic state, by throwing a whole load of video tapes at her, and telling her to get lost. I walked away and never returned. The embarrassment and shame, along with the fact that the industry was a place where everyone knew everyone, prevented me from moving forward within another agency… End of career.

Next, I went into recruitment. Wow – this was great for me. I constantly met new and interesting people, won the company all of their big contracts, entertained clients, and enjoyed the regular office parties. Life was wonderful. I was happy, confident and successful. I had a place on the map. I was a 'someone' in this very big world, but then depression struck me down in 1990.

I struggled to crawl out of this deep and dark hole, falling further and further down at every attempt. I did regain a few years of normality, but could not maintain a level mood for any length of time. Up down, up down – I had no knowledge or suspicion that anything so big and destructive as a diagnosis of bipolar disorder was waiting for me in the sidelines.

The eventual result was that I had a complete breakdown in 1998. Hospital admission after hospital admission. I received a diagnosis of bipolar disorder: my marriage broke down, I lost my job. I temporarily lost my children; I felt as though I had lost my life.

In these earlier years of the onset of my diagnosis, and for quite some time before, I experienced a varied mix of emotions. I have included below a few extracts from my diary which were written at this point in my life, as I was experiencing them.

9 January 2001

I am experiencing so many irrational fears, I feel as though I'm going to be punished for being ill and that my family are going to die because of me. I am feeling an overwhelming sense of loneliness as I cannot identify with any other human being. I am withdrawing from everyone as I cannot explain to anyone what is happening to me. I'm scared, so scared. I feel lost, I don't know where I have gone, what has happened to my life? I cannot sleep and fear the night-time, my head is all over the place, I'm so frightened about responsibility, I want to hide, I want to sleep, my mind needs some peace. I'm writing this at 4am, as sleep is my enemy tonight.

2 February 2001

My counsellor has advised me to do 'nothing', to rest, to take some personal space. There will be no reward in doing 'nothing', it is selfish, bad, neglectful. For that, how can I reward myself?

17 February 2001

I cannot explain my illness to my family as I struggle to understand it myself. Everyone is looking to me for answers. I am feeling so selfish and wonder if this is all self-inflicted. It's all my fault. I genuinely cannot stop what is happening to my mind and body. I try to imagine being 'well' but am so very scared of what the future holds. I am living, on a good day, from day to day, on a bad day, from hour to hour. I do recognize that I have endured a particularly painful and stressful 18 months and as I recount the incidents behind me, I am facing them head on with anger and sadness. I am trying not to dwell on the past but need time to heal. But how long will this take?

19 June 2001

I am giving up hope of ever being well. I am alone in my world of morbid thoughts and feelings. I want to die, I cannot take any more of this pain. The medications I am taking make me feel so 'flat'. I feel so robotic – I am almost numb. I hate the medication, I don't need it, I just want to be back to normal. I need to work, I've never sat around doing nothing. As I write this, I am crying endless tears of loneliness and despair. My fight only exists for my children – I will fight for their life but I am dying inside. I feel as though I have deserted them, and for that I must be punished. They are talking to me, asking questions, but I cannot hear, I'm not listening. I'm trapped within a glass exterior and it is totally sound proof. This is my protection, no one is allowed into my world – this is my only indulgence. I can see out but the world cannot see beyond this glass exterior. This is my life now, a reoccurring nightmare that no one understands. I am fighting to appear normal. I have an excellent mask – my make-up and clothes. But I am walking about naked with tears streaming down my face and a pain so deep within my heart.

July 30 2001

My husband and I have separated. I'm back in hospital because I took an overdose. I'm so scared, confused, guilty. I'm a bad person, how could I have wanted to die and leave my children behind? But I have lost them despite the fact I survived.

The diary entries above show some of the turmoil that bipolar disorder can cause. I now have a love–hate relationship with my disorder. I can only view my manic episodes as a fantastic friend – in fact, the best friend I could ever wish for by far. They take me back to a period in my life when my energies and zest for life were constant.

The depressive episodes of my bipolar can be a far worse enemy. An enemy I resent with every ounce of my being. An enemy that almost literally kicks me to the floor, sending blow after blow, until I cannot get up for the bruising to my mind and body. I can only view the world through a thick pane of glass, I do not belong, I am on my own, a lonely and lost soul. I become a person I detest. I have no value; I lose myself until I lose the will to live.

Bed is my only option during these depressive episodes. The only place I feel safe. I put cushions against my stomach to stop the churning, and a pillow on my head in a feeble attempt to stop the negative thoughts. This is where I stay – this is my life until gradually, my mood begins to creep up. But it doesn't stop there. My mood continues to creep up until I reach a crescendo of mania – my very best friend. I experience such a huge relief – 'Cara is back.'

In reality, of course, Cara is not back. This is the opposite extreme of depression. But it took me some time to realize this. When I am experiencing a manic episode, there are no limits to what I can achieve, or what I am capable of. I run and run at an extreme speed, as though I am running a marathon with no finishing line; my head is in a state of frenzy; my wardrobe expands – spending money on all those items I so desperately 'need': bold colours to match my mood. Hats, shoes, boots, scarves and crazy clothes. It doesn't stop there – there is no end.

The kids 'need' things which have merely been mentioned – these items becomes necessities – I buy them – not only one thing, but everything I can lay my hands on. Must change my car – within half an hour I drive away from the garage, delighted to such an extreme with my purchase. I become reckless on the road, drive at incredibly high speed which is so thrilling. I am dizzy with excitement. I am dizzy full stop. Sex becomes an obsession – addictive. My confidence and ego become huge elements in this crazy place. I mustn't sleep. I don't want to lose the moment. If I sleep, how will I wake up tomorrow? I must keep moving, my mind races with ideas until these ideas become irrational to the outside world. Stopping strangers on the street – talking incessantly – rubbish – can't stop, won't stop – everyone is just so interested in what I have to say.

When I get like this, I need someone to tell me: STOP! Often, it is my partner Basil who takes my mood in hand. At these times, the girls are often scared. He is scared. How much further will I go?

I usually tell myself to turn the music down, stop singing, stop dancing – stop having fun. I resent and resist the suggestion that I need to medicate. I cannot go back to that bleak and dark place. But this is life with bipolar.

There are really only two 'Caras' I'm evoking in the section above: Depressed Cara and Manic Cara. Over time, a real question I've had to grapple with addresses this problem: who am I? Which one of these personalities is the 'real me'? That I will never know. I know which one I prefer, but both are dangerous if I don't behave, listen and take the correct medication for the appropriate episode.

When the cycling eases, I can obtain a level of normality verging on hypomania. I listen, I use medication. I know where I am during each episode. That does not remotely help how I feel. What it does do is help my loved ones to take charge over my mood, guiding me gently through, and gently out of an episode.

This rapid cycling form of bipolar disorder I live with, it depletes my energy – it is a lifetime endurance test and sometimes it feels as though it erodes my soul. At one particular point, not so long ago, I said to my mother that I would rather have a terminal illness than bipolar. Why? Because I would know what to expect the end result to be. With bipolar, during these reoccurring episodes – I have no idea where it will all end.

Living with bipolar disorder: Sandy Knox

Sandy is 45 years old and a single mother who lives in Sussex, England, with her son, Tom, 15. She is a writer and author of a book about bipolar disorder entitled Bipolar on Benefits (I Can't Be The Only One). *I met Sandy in a psychiatric hospital ten years ago, and we have since become very close friends. Sandy suffers from far more depressive episodes as opposed to mania, and does tend to hide herself away from the world during these times, and refers to herself as a 'total recluse'. Despite her somewhat crippling depression, she never fails to have a great sense of humour. I admire her greatly for her devotion to her son and for her fierce determination to achieve her goals.*

Everyone's mood goes up and down, but with bipolar the moods tend to be in the extreme. You're at one end of the pole or the other: on top of the world, over-confident and impulsive, or under a stone, justifying your existence, terrified and aching to die.

Today I'm depressed. The core feeling is flat. Just flat and it's getting worse. It's important for me to differentiate between the illness and how I feel. Depression is an illness; you can't touch it or feel it. I don't feel depressed, I am depressed. What I feel is flat, and that feeling is a symptom of depression. Right now, I feel nothing for anything. Can't stir any emotion. You could tell me anything, anything at all and it wouldn't faze me. Your words would be downloaded to my brain where they'd be filed 'unread'. I'm not dealing with things, I'm bottling them up and in my experience that indicates only one thing – a severe crash, most probably a clinical breakdown looming just over the horizon – who knows?

I can't concentrate on one subject at a time in my head. It's like all these different programs are trying to load at the same time. I need to be defragmented. Then a subject downloads and hits me like a punch in the stomach.

God, no, my dire financial situation. I'm in such a mess. Worry replaces flat. The cloud that my head's in darkens. I smoke and stare, smoke and stare. I can't help myself. I don't know where to start. I'm confused, can't make sense of it.

There's something else that can influence the way I feel. The guilt. It jumps on me out of the blue. Bipolar disorder, manic depression or whatever you call it, does generate guilt in lorry-loads because I let things slip because I can't help it.

I can't keep my standards up all the time, I just can't. So ultimately I let myself and others down. A lot. Hence guilt. And right now at 3.20pm I'm feeling guilty as shit that I've wasted yet another day of my life sleeping and have achieved nothing.

I'm depressed most of the time these days. I pray for a little mania – it would be such a huge relief.

Living with bipolar disorder: Sharon

Sharon is a 42-year-old single mother to Hannah, aged 12, and Jack, aged 11. Both children have written their personal account of growing up with a bipolar parent in Chapter 4, 'Growing Up with a Bipolar Parent'. When I first spoke with Sharon regarding her contribution to this book, she was stressfully awaiting a court case against a very long-standing and trusted friend, who had sexually abused her daughter while he was looking after her. He was recently sentenced to three and a half years in prison, charged on nine counts. Sharon and her children are now trying hard to move on.

Until 2002, I was a successful senior teacher, teaching in adult education, totally unaware of the word 'bipolar', let alone that I might even have it. I had separated from my husband 12 months earlier, and thought I was a happy single mum coping with the everyday life of being a working, single parent, with two children and a messy divorce ahead.

As 2002 started, I was told I had experienced a nervous breakdown and alongside some tranquillizing medication, I was told to rest, avoid stress, and to try to arrange time without my children, by sending them to their dad. My doctor (GP) made it sound so simple. The thought of sorting anything out was pushing me further over the edge.

A week later, I agreed to a voluntary admission to the Priory Hospital. It was heaven to feel safe and secure away from any stress and pressure. I slept for days. Still unaware of bipolar disorder, I was being told that I was under tremendous pressure due to divorce, work, and being a single mum. Just four weeks later it was time to enter the big world again.

I felt fine until I got home and reality set in again. I felt like no one understood me, apart from my next-door neighbour, and that was because she had experienced episodes of depression throughout her life. The children seemed to cope so well as they were young.

Weeks passed, and people thought I was coping well, because I would get up and take my children to school, and even attempt a smile here and there. No one really had any sympathy as time went on. Underneath, I was sinking again. I kept looking at my medication thinking, I just want to go to sleep then wake up normal again, or not wake up at all. That exact thought got the better of me one night when the children were staying over at their dad's. I can't remember how many tablets I took, but I did sometimes wish I'd had the courage to take more.

My children were always there in my mind. Who would care for them and love them? I must have panicked because, in a haze, I told my neighbour. Yes, you know what's next. Accident and Emergency (Emergency Room). I was sent home after my two brothers disowned me at the hospital for my actions. My neighbour was there for me, thank goodness. My children were unaware.

I had a second admission to the Priory, but still no mention of bipolar disorder until a couple of weeks into my stay. I was relieved to have a label/diagnosis. But now I was even more alone with no family to support me, because I now had a mental illness label.

I had two young children, a demanding job that I didn't want to lose, and a damn big mortgage. On my discharge I went home to my two children and tried so hard to manage.

Life was easier to deal with if I had a drink or two. That was all, but sadly my two brothers used this against me, and reported me to social services saying I had a drink problem. When I look back, God only knows how I dealt with that pressure too. One social services visit after another, assessment after assessment, and then I was told I was a good caring mother who just needed the support of a community psychiatric nurse (CPN). I had to prove my sanity for my children's sake.

I had a third and even a fourth visit to the Priory, but since then have been reasonably stable. I put it down to my cocktail of drugs, mainly the lithium. At this point I took early retirement from education and teaching. I did try a couple of times to return, but as soon as I was given any pressure I crumbled.

As far as effects on my children go, it has brought us to be very close together. They are very caring and understanding during my difficult times. I put that down to my CPN and neighbour who have educated them so well. They are registered young carers.

The effects bipolar has had on me in society are very different. I had one particular nasty experience. During my periods of illness, my support network was set up amongst my long-standing friends and my CPN. As you know they are both so important in supporting you through the bad times. Unfortunately one of my most trusted friends abused their position of trust with one of my children, and commenced sexually abusing my daughter.

Thankfully, at 11 years old, she was strong enough to tell her brother, who in turn informed myself. This man, a friend I trusted for over 22 years, has since been charged on nine counts of sexual assault and received a three and a half year prison sentence.

I think in turn this has made me strong as I am so determined to prove that having bipolar disorder does not mean it gives the right to abuse. My CPN is concerned that my inner strength over the last 18 months, dealing with the court hearing, etc., may in turn have an adverse effect. Not a nice experience of bipolar, but it makes you realize, as you go along each pathway towards the trial, how you can and are labelled, in my case, by the defence.

On the same note, the defence have now requested that my daughter is examined, to be labelled 'normal' or 'mad' by the defence to use in court. That is how sad life is for our children in serious circumstances being the child of a bipolar mother.

Living with bipolar disorder: Tracey

Tracey is 44 years old and has been happily married to Rob for 25 years. They live in Swansea with their three children: David, aged 20, James, aged 15 and Bethan, aged nine. David is currently at university, but he returns home frequently and maintains a very close relationship with his parents and siblings. Despite Tracey's severe bipolar disorder, she is one of the most positive people I have got to know, who fills her home with love and laughter at all times. Through writing this book, we have become very good friends. She is an absolute delight to know, has a very contagious sense of humour, and displays a strength of character which I admire greatly. On so many occasions, when I have fallen unwell, she has stepped in and become my very own 'good Samaritan', who continues to offer me her unconditional friendship, support and advice.

Tracey is a devout Christian who has been helped greatly by her religious beliefs, together with the counselling she receives from her church minister.

David, James and Bethan have written their account of growing up with a bipolar parent in Chapter 4, 'Growing Up with a Bipolar Parent'. Rob discusses family life in Chapter 5, 'Adult Relationships and Bipolar Disorder'.

I am 46 years old, the only girl in between two boys. I was born ten weeks prematurely and was always very small for my age. Maybe this affected my confidence, I don't know.

My dad says I was just a normal active child, very talented and able, and that he could see no signs of a problem with me when I was growing up. I had a very good relationship with him.

My mother, however, had severe mood swings, which I blamed myself for. I would hide in a wardrobe when she was on the rampage, and wait there until my dad came home from work. If my mum sent me to bed, I would escape to the church, and pray to be a better daughter. When she was well, however, she was the best mother you could ever wish for. She was the most amazing cook and made me feel incredibly loved. With the benefit of hindsight, I believe that Mum may have been suffering from bipolar disorder, although she never had a diagnosis.

Dad was very funny and lovely, strict but fair, and I never felt threatened by him. He would always praise me and make me feel as if I could conquer the world. He encouraged my talents, and was my saviour, but when I suffered from my first episode of depression, he found it difficult to cope with me.

As a teenager, I became a Christian and got very involved in our thriving church youth group – too involved in fact – I couldn't stop! I got involved in everything going and was never at home. Inside though, I felt very different to everyone else, but could not put my finger on why. I think it was the start of my first manic episode at 18 years old. I had moved to London to start my nurse training at Barts Hospital. Immediately I noticed a change in my behaviour. I was paranoid in class, feeling I had to get the best results all the time, I cried non-stop, often pacing the corridors at night, alone and in tears. My anxiety went into orbit. I had no idea what was wrong. I was depressed! I was impatient, impulsive and extremely edgy. Any day off was terrifying as I needed to be busy to keep my mind from whizzing round. I had to fill every second of the day or I couldn't cope.

I managed to finish my training, but at 21 years old, I experienced a major depressive episode. I thought this was due to the death of my mother 18 months prior to this, and to the fact that 20 months previously my fiancé (now my wonderful husband of 23 years, Rob) had been diagnosed with cancer, which was successfully treated.

I had my first admission to hospital which lasted for three months. I found a good GP who taught me some self-hypnosis techniques that I still use to this day. He mentioned bipolar disorder, but it was never a formal diagnosis.

I had my first son in 1989; there were medical complications that followed his birth, and as a result, I became very depressed and suffered from puerperal psychosis (see pp.31–32). I was admitted to hospital again. This was by far the blackest period of my life.

When we moved to Wales in 1997, I was referred to the psychiatric team as we wanted another baby. I needed to be monitored and I was able to take medication during the pregnancy, and I asked my consultant if I had bipolar. He was very surprised to hear me ask, as it had actually been in my notes since I was 20!

Since being in Wales, I have had a further two three-month hospital admissions to sort out my medication. I was sleeping all the time. One drug sent me into a manic phase and I went on massive shopping sprees that I couldn't control. This devastated my husband Rob and I had to have my credit cards locked away until I had repaid everything. A change of drug made my moods return to normal and I was horrified at what I had done.

My varying symptoms of bipolar are difficult to live with. When I am depressed, I tend to sleep a lot, I isolate myself, I don't answer the front door, I cancel arrangements because I can't face anything. At these times, I have no motivation, I can't be bothered with anything at all, and I keep the curtains closed, go to bed and don't want to see anything beyond the bedroom. My home is my sanctuary.

In the last six months, I have been ill after having an operation, and have hardly left the house on my own. I have become a bit agoraphobic as a result and have limited mobility. I have been offered a way of increasing my mobility so that I can get out more. I have had to do a lot of soul searching over this. Do I want to be more mobile? Am I using my lack of mobility as an excuse to stay in my comfort zone? Only I can answer that, and I have to think very hard about it.

I hate mania with a passion. I feel as though I am driving down a motorway, at 70mph in first gear – my body is not up to doing 70mph. I become restless; I talk and repeat myself a lot, and then can't remember what I have said.

I find a 'mixed state' episode extremely difficult too. I feel high and agitated, I will be up all night cleaning the house, I cannot slow down or rest and I become depressed because I cannot cope. I then cancel all plans and appointments for a couple of days in order to regain control.

When I have experienced psychosis, I have totally lost touch with reality. I have since been prescribed a new medication which helps greatly.

There are times when I 'rapid cycle'. I can be depressed in the morning, but with too much stimulation, I become as high as a kite in the evening. At times, I have not slept for a week. My mood can flip during the course of a day. Sometimes this happens on a daily or weekly basis. During these episodes, my family does not know what to expect from day to day.

In the last two years, I have had a change of medication with great results. This new drug has not cured me, but it has enabled me to take on board the counselling I have been having from my church minister. He is the most amazing counsellor I have ever met. I call him 'the human X-ray machine'. He sees right into the heart and recognizes the problem before I do. He gets me to replace the lies in my head with the truth from the Bible. I have never before been able to 'flip' a depressive episode, but if I meditate on scripture, and bathe my brain it, eventually my mood lifts. I was ecstatic the first time I did this, but now I can do it most of the time.

I am hopeful that I will never be admitted into hospital again.

Living with bipolar disorder: Jo Bell

Jo is 27 years old and lives in Cumbria, England, with her partner, David, and her six-year-old son Malachi. Jo temporarily lost custody of her son during her first manic episode, and speaks about her own experience of the illness, and the struggle she had to regain custody of Malachi. David and Sue, Jo's mother, speak about family life in relation to Jo having bipolar disorder in Chapter 5.

I'm 27, and I was diagnosed with bipolar disorder in September 2007. This followed my first manic episode which resulted in me being arrested (for common assault and possession of cannabis). I was sectioned under the Mental Health Act (1983). I've suffered from SAD (seasonal affective disorder) and depression since I was 15 years old, after my dad hanged himself while severely depressed. With hindsight, he probably had bipolar disorder too.

I'm a textbook case really. My depression displays itself like most people's I presume; I'm tired all the time, I cry a lot, I spend most of my time in bed and I rarely need to, or want to, leave the house. I either eat a great deal or not at all. I have no self-confidence or drive.

The dishes pile up and the house work goes undone. I find it very difficult to socialize and I end up isolating myself.

My mania displays itself with many typical symptoms too. My mind and my speech start racing, I become full of confidence, energy and self-esteem – one year I did all my Christmas shopping in September! I start writing lists and letters for everything. I will wear a skirt and I become very outspoken. I'll spend my days in hospital singing and trying to cheer people up. At one time, I was dancing on the tables in the courtyard!

I was under a huge amount of stress which triggered my first manic episode. I was having problems with my son's father and I was fighting to raise awareness of hyper mobility syndrome (HMS),[2] which is another condition I suffer from. I had just been declared disabled and unable to work, and this sleazy magazine and *The Sun* newspaper printed that I was 'crippled by wild sex', when in reality, I was crippled by the hyper mobility syndrome. Sex sells though.

In the end, I went to a black tie ball in Coventry where everyone suffered from HMS. It was wonderful – each and every one of them congratulated me on my attempts to raise awareness, even if the press had twisted a couple of the articles. I was so relieved that I went 'high' and didn't come down.

When we got home from Coventry, I started cleaning and rearranging the house. My HMS worsened and I started suffering from bone dislocations. I was taken into hospital but no one believed me (there's very little knowledge of HMS in my area). The mental health team was called and somehow I managed to talk my way out of a hospital admission twice. I can't remember much after that, but I tried to self-medicate with cannabis. I was hoping it would calm what I thought was an adrenalin high. I know I went to the local police station to make a statement but they wouldn't interview me. They accused me of being on drugs and when I was searched they found £10 worth of cannabis. I was arrested, bailed, and again sent home. All in all, I was in a state of mania for over a week until finally, the police turned up to take me to hospital. I refused to go and was restrained, sectioned again and taken into hospital.

My son went to stay with his dad, who was granted a temporary residency order. I spent six weeks in hospital as high as a kite. At first I only pretended to take my medication. I didn't think I needed medicating, especially not with an antipsychotic when I had no symptoms of psychosis. It wasn't

2   Muscles, tendons and ligaments are more lax and fragile in people with HMS. The joint laxity with HMS comes with vulnerability to the effects of injury.

until a new doctor explained that I had bipolar disorder, and that antipsychotics also worked as a mood stabilizer, that I agreed to take my medication. I was out of hospital three weeks later.

Thankfully, with the patience of my partner David, we have stayed together even though my bipolar episode had a huge impact on our lives. David and I have a very strong relationship, but last year my depression became so severe that I broke up with him in an attempt to salvage our relationship. It sounds stupid now, but it made sense at the time. It didn't take me long to realize I'd made yet another daft decision, and thankfully he took me back with no hesitation.

Prior to my stressers, triggers and my manic episode, I was a bright, loving mother. I was studying for my degree and, prior to that, I worked as a support worker for those with learning disabilities and the mentally impaired. I trained as a peer educator, and peer counsellor in drugs, alcohol awareness, depression, bullying and teenage pregnancy. I'd trained to work with young offenders at our local prison, and I'm a published poet.

As far as I can figure out, I've had bipolar since I was 15, but it was only picked up as depression until my severe manic episode when I was 25.

Living with bipolar disorder: Phaedra Excell

Phaedra, 33 years old, originates from Illinois in the USA. She moved to England with her husband Mark following a long manic episode, and arranged for her ex-husband to have joint custody of her daughter Amy, who remained in the USA. Phaedra is now living in Southampton, with both her husband Mike and Amy, 12 years old, since recently regaining custody of her daughter.

Prior to my diagnosis, I got my Bachelors degree in English, in 2000, and came very close to finishing my Masters before my first breakdown. When I was in graduate school, I was a single parent, working in two jobs, one of which was teaching two university composition courses, and maintaining an A average in graduate school. It was like I was on fire, totally successful at everything I did. There were bad times, and my divorce from my daughter's dad was absolutely horrible, but I still got through everything successfully. I look back now, and can't figure out why I can't do anything, not even handle a part-time job.

I was undiagnosed until I was 29. From 1999 to 2003, I was basically in a perpetual manic state; I juggled single parenthood with no Child Support (financial support from the government), two jobs, and full-time postgraduate school. When I came down, I came down hard. In a very short time I arranged joint custody of my daughter with my ex-husband and moved from the States, over here to England to be with Mark. We got married in the summer of 2004. I was still undiagnosed.

Since I hadn't finished postgraduate school, and I missed my daughter Amy, who remained with her father at this time, Mark and I agreed that we would go back to Illinois to stay at my parents' house while I attended my last semester. (All of my family and Amy's dad's family lived in the same small town in Illinois.) Things started to go very, very wrong.

Basically I lost control of my mind. Looking back I can't believe I was able to stay out of hospital. I was very out of control. Luckily, I had a doctor (GP) at my university. I'd seen this GP over the years for anything that might be wrong, from sprained ankle to depression and panic attacks. It's difficult to describe how the health centre at the university worked, but I always waited until Dr Dexter was available to see me (a very eccentric thing to do). At any rate, after I had had a very bad fight with my family and had packed my belongings and left, he suggested that I might have bipolar disorder. I was very angry and offended. Sure, things were going badly, but they weren't my fault! They were because everyone else had acted so egregiously! Then, because he was my beloved Dr Dexter (not in a romantic way, but because he was so very wise and kind), I looked into it – and boy, was it spooky – it explained so much about me! I had always thought I was the only one who felt this way.

I really only ever have depression and mania. My depression has made me so ill in the last few years that I'm now begging the health authorities for a proper therapist, because I can't get beyond all of the bad things that have happened in my life. I obsess about embarrassing things I did or said years and years ago, and I can't seem to stop. I'm 33 years old and I still haven't had a full-time job because I just can't handle it along with everything that's whirling around my mind.

I average one manic episode a year, usually in the summer. When I'm manic, I do things which are very out of character. I drink a lot of alcohol, even though I almost never drink at any other time. I'll stay out at people's houses partying while leaving my husband at home alone, which is very odd since we're extremely close. I spend money like it's candy. I have a three-step process regarding buying merchandise. First, I think something is really sweet, then I think it's really cool but it's a bit too expensive (I never buy cheap stuff), and then I become convinced that it's the only thing in the world that will make me happy and that if I buy it, my life will be complete. So I buy it and, needless to say, it doesn't make my life complete. I make grandiose plans, and I can go from being irritable to being violent, shouting and pressuring people to party with me, because I'm totally narcissistic and I think other people are on the planet to make me happy. But I also get more creative, and I'm able to write material for my book, which I eventually hope to get published.

Being bipolar is challenging, even frustrating at times, but I don't think I'd wish to live without it. I've learned to embrace it as a part of myself. I am me. I don't want to be anyone or anything else.

My life's not perfect, but it could be a lot worse. Because of some trouble I had with my sister and my family with regard to my bipolar disorder I'll never really totally trust any of them again, which is a real shame, as we're a close family.

I'm just now at the point where I can function and look ahead, and I've started an Open University degree in psychology. While I know that many psychiatrists are against 'drug cocktails', my psychiatrist has prescribed medication that suits me very well and is a great help.

Living with bipolar disorder: Michael Little

Michael is 28 years old and lives in East Sussex, England. He is single with no children. I have included his account of living with bipolar disorder as I was very impressed with his positive approach to his illness, despite the negativity of his experience. Michael has also contributed to Chapter 6, where he discusses his perception of having a mental illness in today's society.

I was first diagnosed with bipolar disorder in 2003, aged 22 years old. My illness seems likely to have been triggered by a sudden change in personal circumstances and a great deal of stress. I had recently returned home to live with my parents after spending almost two years working for a Christian church as a voluntary missionary. I was filled with emotion about seeing my parents and siblings for the first time in over 20 months. In fact, in retrospect, I was probably filled to overflowing.

It didn't help that I returned with lots of ideas about things I wanted to do and achieve with my life. I had embarked on a full-time course at college, and returned to part-time work, all within a few days of getting home. It very quickly became too much. I began to act strangely. I began to wake in the night and instead of going back to sleep I would concentrate on my studies or reading. Soon, I felt no more need for sleep at all and could go several days at a time without proper rest. Within a matter of a couple of weeks, I had reached the climax of a full manic episode. I was arrested for criminal damage and held in a local cell overnight filled with turmoil and crazed activity.

My life prior to my diagnosis, and before these traumatic events, was somewhat exceptional for a young man. For as long as I can remember I would wake with an extraordinary enthusiasm for the day ahead – full of ideas of what I wanted to do and to achieve. This had led me to travel solo to South Africa, aged just 17, with a suitcase full of charitable donations for the poor. I was to return to Africa a year later, on a trek of the Namib Naukluft desert in Namibia, and in Cape Town I visited a child with AIDS whom I had begun to sponsor.

Meanwhile, I was elected President of my college's Students Union in England, became a local Youth Councillor, and a student member of the college's Corporation. I was always running to meetings and engagements. I had an incessant drive for living and working.

During the earlier months of my diagnosis, I was only really willing to do whatever was necessary for me to leave a psychiatric hospital as quickly as possible. If that meant sitting in front of a tribunal and agreeing to acknowledge that I was ill, I was prepared to do that. But as I began to feel increasingly better, I began to question if I needed to remain on my medication. For a couple of years, I seemed to function quite normally (if a little erratically at times). But recently, I relapsed and was once again quite seriously ill.

Now, these experiences have taught me that I do seem to have a genuine illness, that cannot be easily resolved or ignored. However, I do not feel like a sufferer. Yes, I have suffered. I have had some very traumatic, upsetting experiences because of bipolar. But I do not feel that I have constantly suffered, or that I will always have to suffer. Of course this might also be another form of denial.

But if I am to be entirely honest, no one seems clear about the exact causes of bipolar and, in short, I have no idea where bipolar and I begin and end. So exactly what am I denying or accepting? To what extent does this define who I am, or what control I can achieve? These questions I still ask, and cannot answer. I have little concept of what normality 'should' be.

Living with bipolar disorder: Paul Edwards

Paul is 29 years old and lives in the West Midlands, England, with his wife, Claire. They have no children. Claire appears in Chapter 5, where she discusses her marriage to Paul, and her role as his main carer.

I'm just your usual 29-year-old who was going about his business. I had always been an energetic, over-active child and could be quite boisterous. There were times when my parents would pull their hair out as I would not sleep, and there were other times when the kids at school were literally on the brink of being strangled to death, through no fault of their own. Throughout these 29 years, something lay lurking I never knew about, and it was about to hit me very hard.

Bipolar is not a nice friend. It is your enemy. I can work it to my advantage, but I soon know when I've had enough. My relationship with bipolar is very strained. I can be really hypermanic one minute and then crash down to earth the next, without any warning.

I have a very short concentration span which does not do me, or anyone else, any favours at all. Jobs which I have started have been left unattended and another job started. That's how the cycle goes. I simply cannot co-ordinate what I am doing long enough to stick with it and finish. If I do manage to get it done, it will be in record time as I am in a manic mode.

It's horrible to think that your poor body has to cope with the brain starting one thing and then doing another. One minute I'm happy and the next minute I'm at rock bottom. It all gets too much. Part of my bipolar includes some self-harm. Some people refer to this as a cry for attention. I disagree because the first time I self-harmed, I almost succeeded in actually cutting my wrists. I just couldn't cope any more and wanted rid of this horrible thing. I suppose you could call this a suicide attempt, but I was one of those lucky ones who was found in time.

I have self-harmed 20 to 30 times: nothing as severe as cutting my wrists, but bad enough to notice. I suppose it's a release for the body; I associate it with coming down, if I'm too high or too low. I would never suggest that anybody does this. I'm just saying that I find, sometimes, that it is a coping strategy.

Within bipolar boundaries, there can be a lot of different types of emotions and actions. I tend to get a form of paranoia, worthlessness and agitation. I get tired and want to sleep all the time, or I can't sleep, or won't sleep due to rapid thoughts cycling through my brain. I tend to be a rapid speaker which is yet another symptom to deal with, along with excessive spending.

My wife, Claire, copes very well. She is now classed as my carer and has legal power of attorney for my best interests. She helps me get through my episodes and she will help me by finding me something to do with craft, to keep my hands and mind busy. I may go out into the garden and potter around and do a bit of digging. I also believe in relaxation CDs from holistic shops, to help the brain settle.

At the end of the day, I don't need anything that is too full on the brain, otherwise it will continue going round and round.

Conclusion

In reflecting on my own story and those of the other contributors who feature in this chapter, it's clear that we all experience many common themes and traits of behaviour. Many of us lived almost parallel lives prior to our diagnosis. I have listed below, with bullet points, some of my observations.

- Prior to diagnosis, we all lived a very high functioning life and had successful careers.

- Most of us lived in a state of hypomania prior to diagnosis. Just a few had suffered from deep depression.

- Most of us appear to be creative with a lot of drive.

- Our manic and depressive episodes follow very similar patterns of behaviour: when depressed, nearly all of us become reclusive, spend excessive amounts of time sleeping, crave the safety of our beds, have cripplingly low self-esteem, have felt suicidal, or have made a suicide attempt. One thing in particular jumped out at me – Tracey explains how she could receive help with her mobility, but bravely says that she's unsure as to whether she now wants to leave her 'comfort zone'. So often I have let friends borrow my car and used this as an excuse to stay at home in my 'comfort zone'. Sandy lives a very reclusive life, to the point where she has moved to the countryside where you need transport to go out.

- Our manias display themselves with typical symptoms: pressured speech, raised productivity, creativity, success, excessive spending, making lists of things to do, feelings of conquering the world, raised level of confidence, excess energies, embarrassing behaviour.

- The onset of our bipolar disorder appears to have been triggered by a period of extreme stress and pressure.

- Many of us had separated or divorced prior to diagnosis. Some of us separated or divorced shortly after our diagnosis.

- Some of us lost custody of our children for a period of time.

- Many of our parents, in retrospect, displayed symptoms of bipolar disorder.

- Most of us appear to be sensitive, caring and emotional people.

- Nearly all of us have a lot of guilt issues.

- For most of us, the onset of a manic episode follows stress, too much mental stimulation, pressure, or lack of sleep.

- A depressive episode is often triggered by an upsetting situation.

- Most of us explain that the onset of our bipolar disorder left us with initial feelings of a loss of identity and normality.

- For some of us, our disorder affected our friendships.

- Most of us expressed a feeling of grieving for our past persona.

So, even in just the handful of stories featured in this chapter, it's possible to see clearly the challenges that we all face on a daily basis. All of us continue to fight this illness, but we are all looking at the positive aspects of our diagnosis.

3

Parenting with Bipolar Disorder

Many years ago, I was given a diary entitled *My Hopes and Dreams*. While looking back through my many entries in the diary, I noticed that one of them read: 'I dream that one day, I will write a book, that will help, not only my own children and family to gain an insight into how this dreadful illness can impact on their lives, but other families too.' This book is my attempt to realize this dream, and this chapter is written to convey the feelings, thoughts, viewpoints and coping mechanisms of those with bipolar disorder who have a parenting role.

In this chapter I first include a contribution by child and adolescent psychiatrist Dr Quentin Spender, whom I visited in Oxford at his home. He was extremely helpful and knowledgeable and very friendly, and offered me some much-needed encouragement. Dr Spender considers the effects of bipolar disorder on children and families from a professional's perspective.

Following this is a collection of contributions that focus primarily on the lived experiences of bipolar parents and then in Chapter 4 there is a series of accounts written by children and adults on their experiences of growing up with a bipolar parent.

The effects of bipolar disorder on children and families

Dr Quentin W. Spender

Major mental illness affects not only the person who has it: those around the person are also affected – particularly close family members. Living with a mother, father or spouse with bipolar disorder is hard work. The earlier in a child's development that parental bipolar disorder starts, the more likely it is to have a significant impact on the child's relationship with their affected parent and their development.

Protective factors include:

- the establishment of 'good enough' parenting[3] before the onset of illness

- the formation of strong and healthy attachments to the affected parent, before or despite the illness

- the availability of 'good enough' alternative carers for the child: this could include not only the other parent, but also members of the extended family, supportive neighbours, child-minders, and, if none of these is available, foster carers

- the treatability of the illness: if the lows and highs of bipolar disorder can be kept under control, this will protect the child

- long periods of good health between relapses

- the child's own resilience: being able to cope with difficulties, for instance waiting for Mummy to get better

- strong support networks for the child, including close family members; friends; and teachers, teaching assistants or counsellors at school.

---

3 'Good enough' parenting is a phrase that was introduced by Donald Winnicott (1896–1971; a paediatrician and psychoanalyst) to describe the sort of attention that a child needs to have from a parent, and to emphasize that, as parents, we don't have to get it right all the time. In fact, learning from things that go wrong is part of being an effective parent. (See Rodman, F. R. (2003) *Winnicott: Life and Work*. Cambridge, MA: Perseus Books.)

In these days of changing gender roles, it may not matter so much which parent is affected: the illness of one parent may force the other to become the main carer, and children may feel secure in this relationship. Nevertheless, having a mother with bipolar disorder may be different from having a father with bipolar disorder. For instance, children may identify with the same-sex parent, and either fear being too like them, or take their side in any dispute between the parents. Having an affected father is more likely to result in loss of income, a reduction in living standards and a down-grading house move. Having an affected mother is more likely to result in disrupted or intermittent parenting.

Children may experience a parent's mental illness in a variety of ways. First, the child may witness the symptoms of the bipolar disorder. Second, the child's experience of parenting may be affected. Third, both child and parent may be affected by consequences of the bipolar disorder. Some examples are listed below. Fourth, a young person may (justifiably) fear inheriting the disorder: for any child of a bipolar parent, the risk of developing bipolar disorder is 30 per cent.

How a child can be affected by a parent's bipolar disorder
Witnessing illness

- Seeing a parent constantly in tears or withdrawn, and unable to cope with everyday tasks.

- Experiencing a parent's irritability and emotional unavailability.

- Seeing a parent being manic: for instance, never going to bed; buying lots of stuff; doing bizarre things such as dancing without stopping or cavorting naked; saying bizarre things that the child does not understand.

- Being embarrassed or frightened by their parent's behaviour and other people's reactions.

- Not having any explanation of what is happening (such as people the child has never seen coming round to take Mummy away). An explanation such as 'Mummy is ill' can merely lead to a host of further unanswered questions – although it may help build up hope for recovery.

- Finding a parent in a strange unfriendly place that doesn't look like a hospital.

- Worrying or being distracted in school, and so unable to concentrate.

Effects on parenting

- Feeling insecure or frightened of unpredictable fluctuations in a parent's behaviour.

- Being left unsupervised, or without adequate adult attention, excessively.

- Having to look after siblings.

- Having to look after the unwell parent (this should be the job of other adults, not of the children).

- Not being taken to school regularly.

- Not having things organized for school: arriving without swimming things, gym kit or packed lunch.

Shared consequences

- A reduced standard of living due to the affected parent's over-spending or impaired earning capacity.

- A reduced standard of living due to the well parent having to give up work to look after the ill parent or the children.

- Marital discord or possibly domestic violence.

- Parental separation or divorce – as a consequence of the illness.

- Unwelcome contact with a number of unknown professionals.

Professional attitudes to an adult with bipolar disorder often focus on the individual, and many professionals working in adult mental health services may simply forget to think about the children. This means that not only is the impact of inadequately treated symptoms on children not considered but also, the impact of hospital admission on other family members is not discussed.

Any family member, concerned friend or involved professional needs to make a deliberate effort to see the situation from each child's point of view. Questions to think about in relation to each child include the following:

- What happens to each child when the parent is ill at home?

- What happens to each child when the parent has to be admitted to hospital?

- What sort of relationship does each child have with each parent, including any parent who has left the family home?

- What sort of relationship does the affected parent have with her child when she is well and when she is ill?

- Who are the alternative carers for the child?

  o The other parent?

  o Another relative?

  o Friends?

  o People paid to do this?

  o People found by social services to do this?

- Does the affected parent have friends or a current partner who could be a risk to the child in any way (such as through drug use, domestic violence or sexual abuse)?

- Is the affected parent liable to harm her children in any way? A severely depressed parent may want to kill her children as well as herself. A seriously manic parent may want to involve his children in dangerous escapades. Violence may occur at either end of mood swings.

- Which professional agencies are involved with the family? Examples of agencies that might be involved include:

  o adult mental health services

  o social services

- o police
- o educational welfare service
- o child and adolescent mental health services.
- What is the child's role in the family? What do they have to do more of when the affected parent is ill?
  - o Caring for the unwell parent?
  - o Caring for younger siblings?
  - o Shopping?
  - o Cooking?
  - o Other household chores?
- Who can the child turn to for help?

Sometimes, discussing the importance of the child's needs with an affected parent can have a positive effect: thinking about the child and how they are affected can motivate a parent to seek help for themselves. There is, however, a risk of inducing guilty feelings in any unwell parent: depression leads to guilt about not being a good parent, which worsens the depressive mood. This is where the concept of 'good enough' parenting can be helpful. Most children can cope very well with lapses in parenting, providing they have an explanation they can understand, and providing they have 'good enough' parenting for most of the time.

There may be various other ways in which the family around a parent with bipolar disorder can be helped. Practical assistance can be very important, and may be affordable and relatively easy to arrange: someone to do the cleaning; someone to help get the children to school; someone to be available when they get back; someone to provide regular or emergency childcare. For pre-school children, a day nursery, drop-in centres, or mother and toddler groups may help, or a support network such as Surestart (www.dcsf.gov.uk/everychildmatters/earlyyears/surestart) or Home-start (www.home-start.org.uk). (Please see 'Useful Organizations' at the end of this book for details of organizations based in the US.) Social services family centres can sometimes provide a co-ordinated package of support for a family in need. Older children may benefit from a young carers' group.

─────────────────────

The above provides us with a helpful summary of parenting issues and the effect bipolar disorder can have on children and families from a professional point of view. To complement this, the accounts that follow should vividly bring to life what life with bipolar disorder actually looks like in practice.

Parenting with bipolar disorder: Cara (mother of Georgina, 19, and Tasha, 15)

Georgina and Tasha also contribute to Chapter 4, 'Growing Up with a Bipolar Parent'.

My experience of mothering with bipolar disorder has been, and still is, a constant uphill struggle. Not because my children are particularly difficult; they are not. I believe my struggle lies within myself. Why? Guilt, guilt and more guilt. I tend to over-compensate when I am stable. The girls' lives are then turned upside down when I relapse into an episode.

In 1998, when I first became ill, I found myself totally 'lost' in a world where I had previously felt I belonged. I isolated myself in my bedroom for endless hours and days, having very little input into my daughters' lives. As my mental health spiralled downwards, my marriage came to an end. This was a huge trauma for Gina as she was at an age where she was fully aware of what was happening. Tasha, I would like to think, was almost oblivious, as she was a very 'young' five-year-old.

Gina quickly began to display symptoms of obsessive compulsive disorder and was diagnosed with ADHD (attention deficit hyperactivity disorder). She became very angry towards me yet always wanted to be with me. For a period of time, I had to live with my mother. I went to see the girls every day, but due to being very ill, there were times when I couldn't drive. On these occasions I know the girls felt very let down.

Tasha became very 'cuddly' with me when I was unwell. Gina would scream at me and attack me physically. It was at this point that I realized that she was suffering the consequences of my illness as much as me.

Even though I was painfully aware of Gina's distress, it hit me terribly hard when she handed me a series of pieces of writing to read that she had done. I am including these below, as I feel it important to show the depths of sadness and confusion she was feeling.

Written by Georgina Aiken, just about to start senior school aged 11

One

The crouds around me make me feel so small I feel left out and no one can see me because I am little. I look at my hight level and all I feel that I see are ants and mice and as I look above me I see people. I hate it as I try to talk no one can hear me as if I were an ant. My Life gets ruind over it and my heart feels like nothing it beats and I try not to cry I even hold my breath to stop me crying as I know no one cares for me I sometimes wish I were never born.

Two

As I look around I see so many things I have never seen before. It is so amazing I feel worried. I pause; I take a long look around and just feel like screaming. It's scary and I don't know what to do. I have been to many places that try to help me, it doesn't work I try again, it begins to work and I so on begin to feel a little better and as I look around I feel like I am in a new world. Everything has changed and I feel a new me.

And a happy me as I recognize the things around me and I look at my watch and know the time and that is when I realize I am well.

Three

I AM GOING TO GO ON THE BIG RIDE I AM GOING TO BE BRAVE AND I AM GOING TO FACE MY FEARS. I AM A BIG BRAVE DOG AND I AM NOT GONNA BE SCARED FOR ANYTHING. I HAVE GOT ONE LIVE AND I WANT TO BE PROUD OF THE THINGS I HAVE DONE. MY LIFE DEPENDS ON ME AND I HAVE GOT TO BE BRAVE FOREVER ONWARDS AND NO ONE CAN CHANGE THAT. IF IN MY LIFE ANYONE COULD CHANGE IT, IT WOULD BE ME. I WON'T BE WORRIED AND I WANT PEOPLE TO THINK OF ME AS THEIR HERO AND NOTHING BUT. I WANT TO BE KNOWN IN THE WORLD FOR MY BRAVENESS AND THE WAY IN MY LIFE HOW I SUDDENLY CHANGED. IF I KEEP THIS PEACE OF WRITING FOR A LONG TIME MAYBE, NO ONE KNOWS I MAY BE FAMOUS?

Both girls understood that Mummy was so frequently ill because I had bipolar disorder, and I explained, to the best of my ability, what that meant for me. I also had to explain that there would be times when they had a quieter and sadder mummy than they were used to.

Gina in particular wanted to know how it felt for me as someone with bipolar disorder. She asked me to explain the feelings of being so 'low' and then so 'high'. I thought of myself as a child. I then picked out my favourite memory, which was being in a fairground. I would find it a complete thrill, and my favourite ride had always been the roller coaster. It seems ironic to me now, that I lusted after the thrill of ups and downs. I explained it like this: 'Imagine you are on a roller coaster. One minute you are at the lowest point, which is when I feel depressed and sleep, and cry a lot. Then the roller coaster goes right up, to its highest level, and that is when I develop the thrill of mania. Of course you then drop right down, and that is when the depression returns.' Gina understood this explanation very well and appeared to have a better insight into my mood swings.

Returning to the present time, I make extreme efforts to appear 'well' at all times. It takes a huge fight within myself to achieve this, but I do it for the sake of my children. I will dress nicely when I don't feel up to getting dressed at all, and I make certain I wear make-up at all times. Quite simply, if I do not look after my appearance, the girls immediately recognize that I have become ill.

The pressure I put myself under to keep to prior arrangements with them takes every ounce of energy I have. Today I am not feeling at all well. I am dressed and made up, and I am taking Tasha out after school as planned last night.

Tasha *cannot* be let down. Up until a couple of years ago, she barely noticed my episodes. She was very young when I became ill, and was not exposed to the craziness of my moods. Georgina unfortunately was. During a recent 18-month relapse, Tasha totally lost faith in the fact that I would ever be well again. I was rapid cycling during the course of one single day. I didn't know where I was from hour to hour. I didn't expect the children to know either. Tasha accused me time and again of being unreliable. I was very unreliable. I let her down far too often. She didn't trust me.

Georgina, being that much older, worried herself sick about me. She wouldn't allow me to be on my own at any given time. She adopted a very maternal role. She still maintains that role. She 'wishes me better' every day – even when I am absolutely fine. I assure her that she can now drop that role. I have been well for quite some time. She won't.

I can only refer to my appearance as 'my mask'. I wear this mask to hide my very raw emotions and varying episodes. I wear this mask to 'protect my children'. But sadly, the damage has been done. Gina has not been 'well' herself. Tasha does not believe in me.

Sadly, Gina has had a lot of issues herself, due to the fact that she was a very impressionable age when I was first diagnosed with bipolar disorder and, consequently, separated from her father. There were various other problematic stresses going on around her at this time in her life, which I feel shaped her from a child into an adult far too quickly.

Gina's obsessive compulsive disorder has followed her into adulthood. She suffers from a disturbing number of irrational fears, which haunt her terribly. She has frequent 'vivid and frightening' dreams. She believes these dreams will come true. She carries out various rituals, both verbal and physical, as she feels that these rituals will prevent any harm coming to her or her loved ones. Especially me. She has been in therapy since she was 11 years old. She remains in therapy and is now seeing a psychiatrist.

I am sad to say that, since Christmas 2008, Gina has been suffering from regular bouts of severe depression. I often jump to the conclusion that Gina may have bipolar disorder herself, but this is mainly due to her regular shifts in mood. She can be very fun loving, has a great sense of humour, is energetic and 'appears' to be confident. She has regular outbursts of anger and aggression. When she loses control, she tends to lose her sense of reality – there is no hope, whatsoever, of reasoning with her on these particular occasions. We always discuss 'why' she was angry and aggressive once things are calm. She never knows 'why', and frequently asks me to 'help' her. I have tried to 'help'. She is refusing to take medication. She does not want to be like me. I can understand her fears; medication, to Gina, mean a step in the direction of a bipolar diagnosis.

She is worried about inheriting this illness. The only 'help' I can offer is to treat Gina as I wish to be treated when I am struggling. I hold her tight and close until it passes. She is unhealthily attached to me. She trusts me and only me to 'make everything OK'. Gina may be my eldest child, but to me she will always be my 'baby'. I worry about my child from morning to night. I have stolen a statement from a film (*P.S. I Love You*) I recently watched which I found incredibly powerful. It sums up my feelings in one single sentence: 'The worst thing, apart from losing a child, is seeing your own child taking the same path as you.'

Gina, at times, can be very high maintenance, emotionally and physically. But despite everything, we have a wonderful relationship. We are extremely close, too close. We share the same sense of humour, and are both very childlike. Gina can also be extremely hyperactive. At these times, she likes to 'play'. We play stupid games like pulling each other around the house by each other's feet. We 'play' until we both get out of control and only stop when another family member gets fed up with us.

Tasha is quite the opposite of Gina. She is full of confidence, yet very sensitive. She is extremely 'feeling' and emotional. She is always the first person to go running if someone needs her, or is feeling sad. I have found her crying on many occasions. She explained to me recently that she 'feels others' pains as her own'. I asked her if she would like to read the preface I had written for this book. She did and she broke out into a huge smile. She couldn't believe that I had really written it. We now have a far better understanding of each other then ever before.

Tasha changed school last September, and now has a very wide circle of close friends; two of those friends have a bipolar parent themselves. Her friends often say to me that Tasha is so beautiful, inside and out. She is. It is very reassuring for me that she can confide in her friends. Their parents are also very loving towards Tasha, and offer her their support at all times. They tell me that they love her, and they treat her as one of their own.

Providing I am well, I do the same for their children, all of whom I love so much. Her friends call me 'Mummy Cara'. They are all very affectionate and will lie on me for cuddles, and ask to have their hair stroked. They ring and text me regularly to say they love me, and they often invite themselves over. They love the late-night 'picnics' I make! I do over-indulge my kids with love and affection, and I do the same with their friends. My best medicine is a house full of children.

I feel incredibly proud of my daughters. Although they are totally different in character, they both have lovely natures and show so much empathy for others. They both have clear goals, which we encourage at all times, and they have developed a very good understanding of bipolar disorder. It is especially difficult for them if I am going through an episode. Despite my 'mask', there are other tell-tale signs. If I am depressed, I tend to sleep a lot. I listen to music the children associate with a depression. If I have mania, the music is loud, too loud. I dress differently – alternatively, in bold colours to reflect my mood. I have boundless energy and stay awake until the early hours. Gina will literally march me out of shops to ensure I do not spend money I have not got.

During my 'noticeable' episodes, I strongly encourage the children to live their own lives to the full, and to take themselves away from the situation, if they feel that is what they need. I encourage them to ask any questions they may have, and I will answer them openly and honestly. Tasha will remove herself from the situation by staying with friends. Gina will cling to me.

Both girls resent certain aspects of my illness. They hate my memory loss with a passion. I tend to repeat things, and they become very angry. They do not like the amount of medication I have to take. At times, Gina tells me to stop taking it. I simply explain that I cannot do that.

Despite Gina's own mental health issues, she is a very sensitive, loyal and loving daughter, and sister to Tasha. She has an extremely engaging personality; everyone she meets loves her. She excels in everything and anything she turns her hand to. She has a wonderful and creative flair; she is highly respected at work, and is working towards becoming a successful beauty therapist at college. She has set some wonderful examples of late. Despite her own depression and suffering, she will always attend college, she will always go to work, and she will drag herself out to socialize. I know this is not easy for her. I beat myself up over the fact that if she can do it, so should I.

No words can explain the difficulties I feel about being a parent with bipolar disorder. The guilt attached to my condition is overwhelming. I tend to blame myself for anything and everything. I over-compensate much of the time. I want to 'save' my children from any hurt in their lives. I set myself very high standards, and sometimes almost impossible goals. I fight with myself from morning to night. It is exhausting.

But it is my children who have taught me so much. I learn from their examples every single day. It isn't always about words these days. We all know each other. They can read me from one single look. I can read them too.

There are times, many times, when I just feel like giving up. But these girls keep me going time and again. I look at Gina and Tasha's beautiful big blue eyes, I catch their mischievous smiles, see their knowing gaze, and that makes everything OK.

My children are my world.

Parenting with bipolar disorder: Sandy Knox (mother of Tom, 15)

Sandy's account below illustrates the common problem of 'mother's guilt'.

As if parents don't have enough guilt already. All kinds of guilt. Guilt for things we did, things we didn't do, things we should have done, and things we'll probably never do. My son says he doesn't really notice my manic depression, mind you he doesn't notice much, he's 15! He thinks it's great to have a mum who is mad. A mum who, on the spur of the moment, says, 'Drop everything, we're going to Southend to play on the amusements.' There was also a mystery surprise which I'd organized in a couple of hours; I told him we were going to Cara's, but took him instead to a gorgeous inn on the Norfolk coast for the weekend.

Or I'll take Tom and his mates to Thorpe Park, and use the bluest of language on some of the rides, because I genuinely, honestly believe I am going to fall out. When I'm low he feels for me, I can tell. I explain that I'm not feeling great, and he understands that I will be quieter than usual, sleep more than usual, and sometimes I might cry. But he knows it'll all come right again.

I am a single mother, which is hard. I make every attempt to appear well for my son. I will wake up with my son and see him out the door at 8.10am. I put the radio on to simulate a cheery, cereal-ad-like buzz whilst the Weetabix is eaten and dinner money exchanged. But now I turn it off. It's irritating. It feels as though my life is about feeding, cleaning and laundry. That's all I do. Mind-numbingly boring, repetitive and thankless chores. I can't concentrate on any one subject at one time in my head. I'm in such a mess. Worry replaces flat. The cloud that my head's in darkens. Panic replaces worry. So I return to my bed. My safe haven. Hiding once again under the covers by 9.45am. Hiding in bed again.

I awake at about three o'clock. I'm back to feeling flat again. Back to feeling nothing at all. I feel guilty as hell, having wasted yet another day of my life sleeping, and having achieved nothing.

And now it's 3.20pm, I try to make the house look like I've been up all day for when my son comes in from school. And I pretend I've been so, so busy. More guilt to behold.

Parenting with bipolar disorder: Sharon (mother of Hannah, 12, and Jack, 11)

Hannah and Jack appear in Chapter 4, 'Growing Up with a Bipolar Parent'.

I feel that it is difficult enough growing up for a child in today's society, but to do this at the same time as being young carers puts additional pressures on our children. It is especially difficult when the parent is particularly poorly. People say they understand, but I personally never feel that they do, because unless a person has actually experienced the highs and lows, and seen how it affects their children, they can't truly understand.

My children have often said how alone they feel as carers. They can't talk about their feelings or experiences to the other children in school, for fear of being categorized or bullied. My daughter says it is like living with a time bomb when I am unwell. My community psychiatric nurse (CPN) has been my lifesaver, and relates so well to my children. When I have been ill, they have had no hesitation in ringing my CPN because they know she is genuine. I worry that, one day, one of my children may inherit bipolar disorder. One of the children is so like me.

My children are often late for school, due to me not being able to get myself going, or actually being ill. Amazingly, despite time absent from school for various reasons, both children are outstanding achievers in school. My son not only achieves academically but also plays for the local football team.

The care Hannah and Jack offer is variable depending on how low my mood has taken me. It can be anything from getting themselves up and fed and watered just with my presence and no physical Mum input, to perhaps brewing and seeing that I eat. They make regular contact with our network of support. Hannah has often made important calls to report my needs for help to my CPN. To them it has become part of their everyday life that they sometimes have to put into practice. Both children understand that sometimes they might just need to sit and have a brew with me.

Parenting with bipolar disorder: Tracey (mother of David, 20, James, 15, and Bethan, 9)

David, James and Bethan appear in Chapter 4, 'Growing Up with a Bipolar Parent'.

I still struggle with this awful illness – on a daily basis at times. I find it difficult to get out of bed. I will get up and see the kids off to school and then, instead of getting dressed and getting on with the day, I will hurry back to the safety of my lovely bed – my best friend. I just want the day to go away while I am asleep. I don't know why I do it, but the effort of getting washed and dressed is just too much on those days. My nightmare is to have to stay up and wait for a delivery or a workman coming round to do some work on the house. Then I can't hide and have to get up. The silly thing is that, once I get going, I usually enjoy those days. If I have a blank day in my diary, oh, what a joy! I know I can go back to bed and not be disturbed. The curtains remain closed, and the phone goes unanswered.

When the children come home from school, I either pretend I have been busy all day and need an hour's rest, so I can go back to bed, or I manage to stay awake and pretend I have had a good day. The guilt I feel for doing this is enormous. I am a total waste, but on those days, I just can't help it.

When I go to the other end of the spectrum, I am up half the night doing jobs that don't need doing, cleaning, washing, writing endless lists – anything to make up for the jobs I didn't do when I was in hibernation. The trouble with that is that I can get exhausted and then my mood will crash down again. This awful illness has taken away my natural braking system. I have two speeds – fast and stop.

As a parent of two sons aged 20 and 15, and a daughter of nine, I feel guilty that I am sometimes a burden to them. I said to my 15-year-old son yesterday that I felt guilty that he had not had any extra-curricular activities outside of school because I was too unreliable to get him there every week. He replied graciously with a huge smile and a hug, 'But, Mum, that was out of your control, you were ill but you have taught me all about the Lord, and shown me how much Jesus loves me, and my faith will carry me through my life. You also noticed before any doctor did that I was autistic, and you worked so hard to bring me out of my silent little world. We are now very close and have such a laugh together, Mum.'

I am blessed to have three such exceptional children that I don't deserve, but God has given me by his grace. I do have moments when I fear that the bipolar may have been passed down to one of my children, either genetically, or by one of them copying my actions. I will just have to leave that worry with God to sort out, as that is beyond my control.

I do feel embarrassed when I look at other mums, and realize I don't do as many things with my kids as they do, or come up to their standards. I am unreliable as I am at the mercy of my moods from one day to the next. My 15-year-old son said, 'Don't worry, Mum, you may have fallen short in some areas, but in others you have excelled. Your cooking is amazing, and we always feel loved and appreciated, even when you are down.'

I hate this illness, and would much rather lose a leg and hop round on crutches. I hope I haven't passed it down to any of my children. I can't see any signs of it yet in any of them. I wish I wasn't such a burden to them, especially to my husband, Rob. He takes so much on his shoulders when I am ill, and rarely moans, but is just happy when I surface again as my normal self from an episode of being unwell. He deserves a medal for putting up with me for 25 years and won Carer of the Year for our region presented by The Wave and Swansea Sound radio stations in 2007, after I nominated him – an honour that I feel he deserves, and one that he just gets embarrassed about. Jesus said, 'Come to me all of you who are heavy laden, and I will give you rest.' I find that to be true every day of my life. I don't know how people cope without Christ in their lives. Let alone when bipolar is thrown into the mix!

Parenting with bipolar disorder: Karen Paige (mother of a daughter, 14, and a son, 10)

Karen is a single working mother to a daughter of 14 and a son of 10. She has struggled to accept her bipolar diagnosis, and tends to keep her feelings to herself where possible. She speaks openly and honestly throughout her account, and discusses the difficulties of coming to terms with a mental illness, due to a general lack of understanding of the illness and its negative portrayal in society.

I don't think that I am always a good role model for managing feelings. I have to try so hard at times to keep things in so that I can function, and so that they don't spill out. At times I feel too tired to cover up. I want to protect my children, and not put too much on them, particularly as I am a single parent. I think it rubs off on them a bit at times, and maybe we don't talk about feelings as much as we could and just get on with things instead.

I find it hard to talk about being bipolar as it makes it more real when you say it aloud. I know when I have been hospitalized, those looking after the children have said something to them, but I'm not sure what. You would think that I would have checked it out, but it is so painful.

I have tried more recently to acknowledge the whole bipolar thing more openly, but for me it's a process of acceptance, and this probably explains why I have been slow in being more open with them about it, as I still find it hard to get my head around the diagnosis. I was surprised, during a very recent major manic episode while on holiday, by how OK the kids seemed. I openly acknowledged that I wasn't myself and couldn't think properly. It was obvious to them that this was true, and that their normally very capable mother just couldn't get her head around simple things, and kept wandering off in her mind.

While it was a fine line, I had insight that they knew I wasn't right. They didn't seem too worried by what was going on with me, but they recognized that this was not dealt with very well by my parents, who were also on holiday with us. I think the kids knew I would get it under control, and that it would be OK, as they have seen it all before.

When my illness has only meant hospital, with no explanation, then it's very confusing for them, especially with all the weird stuff that happens before such a crisis point is reached. But now that we've been through blips together, and worked it out at home, I think they trust the fact that it will pass. Ultimately, in terms of trust, especially for my son who is very close to his dad, I do feel sad that I cannot consistently be a person he can trust. His dad is a very part-time absent father, but at least my son can always rely on his sanity and sound mind.

Discrimination is a topic in our house. We do have discussions about how people with mental illness can be viewed negatively. I try very hard to appear 'normal' to their friends when I am not feeling right, and can get paranoid that I'm not keeping up appearances properly. When I was last in hospital, my daughter told only her closest friend. The kids do know about negative views of people with mental illness, and to protect them from this directly impacting on us, I encourage them to keep it within the closest circles.

My experience of single parenting is that the kids tend to be more independent and responsible than in two-parent families. I don't think my children feel responsible for me. It was only three years ago that I was diagnosed, although the onset followed the birth of my second child ten years ago. I don't think my diagnosis has really changed the dynamic in the family in terms of responsibility. Sometimes my mother says that my son is too old for his years. He does seem to be very switched on to me, and likes to be around me a lot. He's pretty smart, and maybe does help me think through things.

My daughter is different, less interested in spending time with me, as she is a teenager, but also, similarly, she can take charge of certain things. I worry that the kids might think they are responsible for me when I am unwell. People might tell them to behave and to help me when I am not myself. Expectations of others are certainly greater on my daughter – the eldest child. I worry about who will care for my kids if I am ill. I have ultimate responsibility, and it's not that easy, as my network is not huge. It feels as if I can't get really ill, as there is no good alternative option for them.

I was in hospital when my daughter was in the first year at secondary school. My son went to his dad's, but a friend cared for my daughter, and things were a bit all over the place. I don't know what was said to her, and I was at the stage of not really believing the bipolar thing was true and not wanting to talk about it. She also had to be looked after when I gave birth to my son and had to stay in hospital as I developed puerperal psychosis (see pp.31–32).

We did run into problems with my daughter when she was 11 years old and I believe that this was associated with me being unwell. In a nutshell she had had to grow up very quickly. When I came home from hospital, I didn't realize how much growing up she had done, and related to her as the 11-year-old she had been before I left. She rebelled, and it was hard to find common ground. She turned her anger inwards as well as having explosive displays. We did resolve these difficulties. I feel really sad that she had to grow up quickly, and wish that there had been an alternative arrangement when I had been unwell, where she could have been cared for better. I am aware of some of the situations we have been through and worry about the cumulative effects of any adversity. I worry as well that my keeping a lid on feelings is not the best way to equip my children for the future.

Parenting with bipolar disorder: Jo Bell (mother of Malachi, 6)

When I was first diagnosed following my first acute mania and subsequent sectioning, Malachi was only four and, thankfully, a little too young to understand what was going on around him, but I have no doubt it's had an effect on him.

I've had over 12 years of experience of my depressive episodes and I've became a pro at managing them and hiding their effects from all but my partner, David. The mania, on the other hand, was totally new to me. At first it was the rapid speech which was stranger than anything, or it was to begin with anyway.

Then I stopped sleeping and eating. My thoughts became irrational and they were going a mile a minute and by the time Malachi went to his dad's for the weekend, I was really losing touch with reality. I was hallucinating and having delusions of grandeur and I was really starting to worry my fiancé, David.

I knew something was wrong but I didn't know what. I phoned Malachi's dad and told him Malachi had to stay there, I couldn't have him back. It didn't go down well and we argued on the phone. A few hours later, when he turned up to pick up Malachi, he saw the state I was in and accused me of drinking and doing drugs. He told me I was an unfit mum and that he was applying for custody. I was devastated but still high as a kite. The symptoms worsened and after a major panic attack (where I had chest pains and couldn't breathe), an ambulance was called.

Once at the hospital, the mental health team were called without my knowledge, but then again, even if they had told me, I wouldn't have remembered. I was a mess. I couldn't sit still, couldn't string a sentence together, but couldn't stop talking. I hadn't slept in eight days. I was assessed, given sleeping tablets and after six hours with the team, I was offered a bed on the mental health ward. I was positive I'd be fine if I could just sleep, so I refused. Eventually to the amazement of my fiancé, I was taken home. They checked up on me every three hours the following day, but after a while, I lost the tiny fragile grip I had left on reality and stopped answering the phone. Next thing I knew there were four people on my doorstep wanting 'a chat' with me. Two hours later I was told I was being sectioned and refused. They sent for the police and I wasn't thinking straight so I fought back, leading to me being pinned down and restrained.

During the episode, I was adamant that the sectioning was down to my mum and because of that, my fear and anger were focused directly on her. I'd like to take this opportunity to apologize for that. Thinking back, I am so glad that Malachi didn't witness any of this, especially the part where Mummy was thrown into the back of a police van and taken to hospital. Unfortunately I was in hospital for six months and it wasn't until I came down from the clouds that I saw the devastation I had caused. Malachi's dad had filed for temporary custody and it had been granted. I had lost my son and I missed him so much it physically hurt. He was my life and he was gone.

The depression that followed my high was the deepest I'd ever known. I didn't leave the house for three months, I didn't get dressed, didn't open the curtains, I slept a lot and cried the rest of the time. I was fighting to ignore the suicidal thoughts and I really wanted to self-harm but I didn't. Eventually, with the help of my fiancé and the social worker I was assigned when I was discharged from hospital, I crawled, slowly, out of the depths of my dark depression and started focusing on how to go about getting my son back. It took months. I had to be well before the authorities would even contemplate it and that took some time. After having no symptoms of depression or mania for three months I started the process of jumping through hoops, for both the courts and Malachi's dad. I saw my psychiatrist every six months and my doctor (GP) once a week as requested; I took my tablets (olanzapine) religiously and I tried as best I could to get on with my life.

After seven months of Malachi living with his dad, the courts allowed me weekend access, and two months after that, Malachi was allowed to come home again. Finally my little boy was back and I was so pleased. I regretted dreadfully everything I'd put him through. He'd lived with me all his life, then suddenly, without warning, he was shipped to his dad's and then brought back nine months later. That was a lot to deal with at such a young age and it's definitely had an effect on him. His behaviour at school deteriorated and he started lashing out at other children. Thankfully we're on top of that now but we believe it's been due to the trauma of what he's been through.

Malachi is now six and he knows that I have bipolar disorder. We represent mood swings with the characters out of Winnie the Pooh: Eeyore is depressed, Pooh is stable, Tigger is hypomanic and dresses in a jester's outfit with bells on when he is manic. Malachi knows how I'm feeling because I'm acting like one of the characters, and it's easy for him to understand. He doesn't know much about the illness itself and that's the way I want it for now as I feel he's still too young to take much more onto his shoulders. He knows I was 'ill' and that's why he went to live with his dad, and he knows it was bipolar but that's about it. Thankfully, since starting medication, I've only had little ups and downs, and none of them lasted more than a couple of days.

Is it difficult to parent with bipolar? Yes. But that doesn't stop me from doing it. I love my son dearly and David and I want to give him a brother or sister one day soon.

Children have a wonderful gift of winding parents up something chronic, knowing just which buttons to press. Unfortunately having bipolar disorder means this can be a trigger and it often is. These days I'm really good at catching my episodes – as soon as I feel triggered, I up my medication and I'm all right after a day or two of sleep, but with me doing this, David has to pick up the slack while I rest, and that's a lot of pressure for him sometimes. I find the hardest parts are the school parents' evenings, assemblies and sports days. I really struggle with crowds and David has to come with me so I can manage being there at all. But no matter how bad it is for me, I'm always there. Malachi is my son and is the most important person in my life. I refuse to let him down as I did when I was ill.

Some little things are hard too, like getting out of bed to get him up and ready for school. So far we've never been late but, because of the meds, I'm always really tired and I have to have two alarms to get me up. School holidays can be a nightmare. We always have a bunch of Malachi's friends round and that in itself can be very tiring. I can manage three to four days of it, but then I have to have a day off and get some sleep on the sofa, so again, David has to take over.

There's also a slight problem with discipline as I'm not as consistent as I'd like to be. When I'm 'up', I let Malachi get away with more than I should. I do it when I'm low as well, but for different reasons.

I often feel guilty that I'm not like other mums but I know Malachi loves me and that makes it all worthwhile.

Parenting with bipolar disorder: Phaedra Excell (mother of Amy, 12)

In November of 2008, I went to the States to see Amy and stay with my family, as usual. But her circumstances had changed: her dad had a new girlfriend who seemed determined to sabotage any good relationship we had regarding Amy.

Worse, the girlfriend and her two sons, aged 11 and 13, had moved into the little two-bedroom house where Amy and her dad lived. Not only that, but they had all three children sleeping in the same room, Amy on the top bunk, one of the boys on the bottom bunk and the other one on the floor. I found out about it when Amy's dad (drunk, as usual) rang me and started to harass me – he accused me of threatening to take him to court for custody, and listed a whole litany of things that I was supposedly upset about. Two words caught my attention: 'shared bedroom'. I asked Amy and got the truth out of her. I then called her grandma, who I am quite close to, and asked her just what the hell was going on. She told me that it was time for me to take the reins, and get Amy out of that hellhole.

So, ironically, Amy's dad ended up provoking the very thing he had falsely accused me of planning. The new girlfriend is a real piece of work – hardly a month goes by without her being arrested for assault or illegal driving or whatever. So I got a really tough lawyer, and said that if it took £10,000 to get her back I was prepared to spend it. All told, that's about how much it did cost.

While all the legal wrangling was going on, I stayed in the States, keeping Amy by my side as much as I could. Things didn't settle down, they got worse. The cops got involved, and for a while I carried a handgun everywhere I went. At one point, her dad's girlfriend would call me from her work and harass me, accusing me of being on drugs, etc. It was a strange thing for her to say, since the town's chief of police had told me outright that he knew *she* was involved in drugs. So I offered to pay for all of us to have urine analyses, and she hung up on me and never mentioned it again. But she did tell anyone who would listen that I was calling her at work and trying to get her into trouble. When Amy's grandma told me that, I laughed and said I could very easily get all the phone records for every phone I had access to, and I could prove that I had never dialled that number. She stopped calling me after that message was passed on. I got a lot of support from the local authorities, and Amy's teacher was very helpful.

All of this produced a lot of chaos, which seems to act as a flashpoint for my bipolar disorder to kick into high gear and start causing trouble. It was very hard to keep it all together, and I think the only reason I did was Amy. I didn't want to scare her more than she was already scared, and she definitely didn't need two parents going off the deep end at the same time. All the same, it was hard.

And when I felt like giving up, when I was desperate and tearful and frightened, Amy was the brave one. She kept me going, refusing to let me succumb to the darkness. She would remind me that we weren't just doing this for ourselves, we were doing it for my husband Mark, too – Mark, who was all alone back here in England, feeling helpless, unable to protect his wife and her daughter. Amy would say that we had to get back to Mark, that when we did everything would all be OK. And she was right. It's when she's visiting her dad in the States that I worry. It doesn't help that her dad does things like 'forget' her passport so that she has to fly back a day late after I scramble to sort it out with the airlines.

Basically, her dad tried to bully me into backing down, but I had both money and a just cause and knew I wouldn't lose if it came to going to court. He didn't have any money, and I think his lawyer probably told him he would lose. So in exchange for my signature on a 'quit-claim' (a simple document giving up ownership of a house) regarding the crappy two-bedroom house, he gave me my baby back. It was the happiest moment of my life.

But being a bipolar parent is hard; I often fly off the handle and get very angry about little things, and I know it bothers Amy. I always carry a world of guilt around, especially when I'm upset or ill and our roles are reversed, with my ten-year-old seeming more like the parent, fussing over me, cuddling me, whatever she thinks I need. But I know she's happier here – unlike her dad and his girlfriend, Mark and I never fight, and we don't drink alcohol or do drugs. She always knows what to expect from us: unconditional love and attention. But I still feel guilty.

For example, I was diagnosed with hypothyroidism (an underactive thyroid, which, I found out, is often linked to bipolar disorder) late last year, and I was so exhausted all the time that I decided to go off *all* of my psych meds in an effort to isolate what was causing my chronic inertia.

I've been OK without the meds, mostly, but when I feel hopeless or angry I always wonder if I should be back on them. I hate the zombie feeling I get with them, but I feel so overwhelmingly guilty for putting Amy through all my moods – she definitely bears the brunt of them, and I know it's not fair. My mother was clinically depressed throughout my teenage years, making a confusing time all the harder, and I really don't want to put Amy through the same.

I've waited seven years to have her to myself, and I'm so grateful to have her that we never do anything without her – I've never left her with a child-minder while Mark and I do something alone. Even if it's Valentine's Day, she goes out with us. And that's how I want it. For years I desperately yearned to have the family I dreamed of, and now that I have it I'll never let it go. So I guess in a way, even with my ups and downs, I force myself to keep it together for my daughter. She lived in hell for a year, afraid to tell me because she didn't want me to be hurt, and I feel like I have to make it up to her.

I'm honest with her about my bipolar disorder – I tell her it's like a tap: when I feel sad, it's dripping, and when too much is whirling around in my head, the tap is on full blast. I try to make sense of it for her, and I am constantly haunted by the thought that I might have passed it on. So far I've been lucky – she's a normal kid, braver than I could ever be, intelligent and sensitive. So I do everything with her in mind.

My mother wasn't honest with me about how she was feeling, and I think it would have made a big difference to me if I had known that she wasn't angry with me personally, she was just having a hard time of it. But I do find myself apologizing a lot to Amy, and I'm always afraid I'll end up pushing her away unintentionally.

We talk about my brain as if it were a separate person, as in, 'My brain's feeling sad today.' It helps us all distinguish between the real me and the other me who's being kicked around by a disorder I can't control. I'm very careful to emphasize that I can't control it very well, and sometimes it goes its own way. It's not anyone's fault if they don't feel well, and you never know what's going on in someone else's life – all the more reason for humans to cut each other some slack. Bipolar disorder not only affects the way I live, it affects the way I see the world – if I can be in so much pain and hide it, isn't there a chance that others are hurting too, and just need a little kindness to make it through the day more easily?

Discussing a parent's bipolar disorder with the children

From the stories above, it's easy to see how young children as well as teenagers can often be confused about their parent's disorder. There could be many questions they are looking for answers to, and parents can deliberate over if, when, where or how they can explain their diagnosis to their children. In my opinion, it is vital that all children, despite their age, have a clear understanding about the disorder.

When you are explaining bipolar disorder to a child, it is important that it is clearly and tactfully explained, gearing the answers to the age of the child. Written information about the disorder can be very useful. It is worth explaining that the disorder is not curable, but can be controlled with medication. The child should not be misled in a way that could ultimately lead to disappointment. It is also wise to explain that, despite medication, episodes can still occur.

Explaining clearly how the parent feels during the varying episodes could well equip the child with the knowledge of signs to look out for at the onset of an episode. If they understand the different episodes that their parent may be experiencing, they may then be able to ask more questions about how the illness affects the parent, and express how they feel during each episode. Encourage them to speak to a family member, a carer, or the doctor looking after your condition. It is important to reinforce the fact that the child should always be able to talk to someone during these times. Children can feel an overwhelming sense of responsibility, even blaming themselves for your disorder, so close contact with someone they trust is essential. It is vital to have a plan of action in place to assure your child is catered for, should life at home become too traumatic or, of course, should the parent be taken into hospital at short notice.

Sometimes the child might experience feelings of anger, sadness, fear and confusion. They may not talk to the parent about their feelings, so as not to upset them. Assure the child that you are always interested and willing to discuss how they feel. Explain that despite your illness, ultimately, you are their parent and love them, and that you are always there to listen.

Quite often, the child's feelings are overlooked by the professionals. To enrol the support of the doctors, psychiatrists and social workers for the child, the parent and child should attend appointments together so that the child can voice their feelings and concerns. Perhaps the doctors, along with the parent and child, can discuss an action plan should the child become overly concerned or scared.

The child cannot be sheltered from the fact that their parent has bipolar disorder, but it is important to take every measure to avoid making it any harder on them than it has to be.

Conclusion

In this chapter, there are many common factors to how we feel in our role as bipolar parents. Looking at everyone's stories, including my own, the following observations can be made:

- Every mother has expressed extreme feelings of guilt for how their bipolar disorder has affected their parental role.

- Most of us have spoken about our fight to appear 'normal' and 'well' despite the difficulties we are experiencing.

- We all feel concerned and sad about how our bipolar disorder affects the children.

- Most of us speak about our regret that our children have had to grow up prematurely, and our sadness that, at times, our children take on the parental role.

- Many of us discuss the fact that our children no longer trust us due to the inconsistency of our moods.

- Some of us recognize our children are possibly showing signs of inheriting bipolar disorder and express our fear about this.

- We all find it difficult parenting with our bipolar disorder.

- A lot of us over-compensate when we are feeling stable.

- All of us have discussed our bipolar disorder with the children in order to give them a better insight into our condition.

- Many of us have difficulty in getting up with our children in the morning due to our medications, and speak of our struggle with those guilt issues, especially when our child is late for school.

- All of us speak about how our children have kept us going.

- Most of us now recognize that our children accept and love us very much despite our bipolar disorder affecting their lives.

For further support, contact your local bipolar disorder support organization – some useful addresses and resources are included at the back of this book. One leaflet I have found particularly useful, directly written for the child who has a bipolar parent, is *Why Did My World Have to Change?*, which is available in the UK from MDF The Bipolar Organization, but there are other great resources out there.

4

Growing Up with a Bipolar Parent: The Children's Story

Since developing bipolar disorder ten years ago, at the age of 35, I have painfully and often helplessly observed my own children, Gina and Tasha, going through the roller coaster ride of emotions which attaches itself to bipolar disorder. I have seen the horror on both my daughters' faces in reaction to my manic and depressive episodes. Through the years, I have found little, if any, literature or outside help on offer to support the children. This has given me the courage and fierce determination to write about the subject.

There are so many children growing up with a parent who suffers from bipolar disorder, and having researched this in great depth, I have discovered that most of them, if not all, suffer from an element of difficulty connected to their parent's illness. To say I feel incredibly passionate about how mental illness can touch the lives of so many families is truly an understatement.

During the research undertaken to write this book, I developed a keen interest in also interviewing a selection of adults who had been brought up by a parent with bipolar disorder. Some of them have inherited the illness themselves, and discuss this within their personal accounts, which I have included in this chapter. I have used all of the personal experiences in their entirety to represent fully how mental illness in a parent has shaped each individual on their path to maturity.

The children of parents interviewed for this book, who range from nine years old upwards, have also contributed to this chapter. They each individually discuss their experience, their role in the home, and their understanding of living with a parent who has bipolar disorder.

Having taken into account that there are so many different aspects and symptoms of the illness, I have had to make the very difficult decision to use only a small selection of personal experiences, from both the children and the adults, that best illustrate a broad insight into the feelings and effects that their parent's disorder has had on them.

I owe huge thanks to all the people who have willingly contributed their viewpoint for this chapter and, of course, to the parents, for permitting me to include their children's accounts.

Growing up with a bipolar parent: the experiences of children

Growing up with a bipolar parent: Cara's children

I have already written my account of parenting with bipolar disorder in Chapter 3; it has been very enlightening, but terribly sad, to read how both Gina and Tasha, at their current ages, feel they have been affected by my illness.

Despite this, I feel that we all have a better understanding of each other's feelings, and we have each made a promise to air our emotions during these difficult times. We share an exceptionally close relationship and, despite my bipolar, our home is always filled with love and laughter.

Georgina Aiken, 19 years old (written between the ages of 17 and 19)

I was about ten years old when my mum got noticeably unwell, although I now know that in about 1998 she was beginning to get unwell as our dog, Yanni, passed away and that is when it started.

My mum and I have always had an honest and close relationship, and my mum has always told me everything.

At the time I recognized my mum was not herself, I was in the last year of primary school. At this time things were becoming more difficult in the sense that my mum was becoming lower and lower. Primary school was coming to an end and I was starting secondary school. To add to it, my mum and dad told me they were separating.

To me, at the age of ten, things couldn't possibly get any worse. My mum and dad *never* argued, primary school was the best time of my life and Mummy was ill. I couldn't understand why my family seemed to be coming to an end. All Mum and Dad kept telling me was, 'We just don't love each other as much any more.'

I can't remember exactly when, but soon after they told me, my mum became too ill to stay at home, and got admitted into hospital. All I knew was that Mum was 'ill', I didn't know how, why or what with. Daddy took me and my sister Tasha to visit Mummy in hospital regularly, but it made everything about my life feel so insecure.

My mum came out of hospital about six weeks later but said she couldn't come home. She had to stay with Nana for a while. Nana, at the time, lived about half an hour away and I didn't see Mummy often. Whilst she was there, all I was concerned about was when Mummy was coming home.

She didn't come home. She rented a small one-bedroom flat near to where my sister, my dad and I lived. I knew then that Mummy and Daddy had split up and I couldn't come to terms with that for a long while. I just expected them to get back together some day, and reassured myself that would happen to make me feel more secure.

When I went to stay with Mummy in the flat once a week she would tell me everything. Sometimes she told me too much and I didn't want to hear some of the things I knew. I understand she was unwell and she also regrets telling me some of the things she did.

I was only 11 at this time and it all became too much.

During this time, living with my dad was not easy in the slightest. He had developed depression himself since Mummy and he had split up.

Mummy was ill and not in a fit state to look after Tasha and me, so I had to deal with it while no one ever knew.

I remember one night I plucked up the courage to go downstairs and Daddy couldn't even talk. I picked the phone up to ring Mummy and he grabbed it away from me. Mummy wouldn't have been able to drive though.

I ended up lying in the side of Daddy's bed where my mum used to sleep, with headphones in my ears as loud as they could go. This was to block out all the noise until Dad was safely in bed so I could go back to my bed.

Mummy had been in and out of hospital regularly and she came out one of the times and told me and Tasha that she had met someone. I had met him before when they were just friends and Mummy and Daddy were still together but now they were dating. My reaction was horrific – I was so sure Mummy and Daddy were going to get back together that I couldn't believe this awful news. I refused to meet him for months on end. He even bought us all tickets to see *Fame*. I didn't go.

Long after, the rest of the family explained that Basil was helping Mummy and was very supportive and that he was not the monster I imagined him to be. I agreed to meet him and realized after a while that he genuinely was making my mum feel better. But I felt sorry for my dad as he had no one.

Amongst all this, I then found out I had got into the secondary school I least wanted to go to. I cried for days. Mummy agreed to appeal to get me into the secondary school that all my friends were going to. By this time Mummy was on the mend.

On the day of the appeal Mummy moved into a house which was in the catchment area of the school and on the same day Daddy moved into a smaller house. I got into the school I wanted. The houses they moved into were lovely.

My mum would not only get low and depressed – when she moved I noticed a different side to her. She went extremely high. I always knew when she was going high because I would come home from school and all the furniture would have been moved around and there would be presents for my sister and me. It was all spend, spend, spend when she was high and there was no control.

I started staying with Mummy more often but there were times when I couldn't stay for weeks on end because Mummy was too ill to look after me.

I developed a number of different obsessive compulsive disorders and rituals about now and one main one was a ritual saying, 'night night, love you, see you in the morning', a number of times, to everyone in the house. I would have to make sure that the person I was saying it to repeated it back to me last. I also couldn't stop washing my hands.

During this time, due to my dad's depression, I couldn't stay there. Tasha and I moved back home with my mum, but she was still ill so Basil mostly took care of my sister and me.

Because of the problems at home, my school work was terrible and I was at school for no more than three days a week due to upset and stress. I hated school and although I had wanted to be there, I didn't any more. I wanted to go to a new school which was an hour from where we were living and start afresh. I wanted to be with all my friends from that area. After a while Mum let me change schools and by Year 9 I was at a school where I felt much happier.

Life at home also began to get easier. My dad received counselling for his depression and Mum was well for longer periods of time due to the medication she was on.

For about three years Mum remained more stable with the exception of a few short episodes of being high or low. My mum's bad patches when she's unwell can last a day, a few days, weeks, even months, but it makes us appreciate her even more when she's well, and when she has gotten over her bad patch, she is well for a much longer period of time.

When my mum sleeps less, eats less, has more energy and spends more money, it's usually a sign that she's going high. The symptoms of both mania and depression are quite distinct, although I often mistake little things that are nothing for symptoms of depression or mania. When my mum's manic, it's as if someone has pressed a fast forward button on her and she has super powers to do the impossible, which is scary, because she really does believe she can do anything, and I feel like everything needs to be out of her reach. When she is depressed she stays in bed most of the time, or cries to her friends on the phone. I get very frustrated when she's depressed because I want to be able to do something to change the way she is feeling but I know I can't.

I cannot have a proper conversation with my mum when she's unwell because I end up upset when I see her not being herself. I feel as if I lose a huge part of normality and nothing goes right until she is better, as her being unwell is at the back of my every move until she is OK again.

My mum has learnt to know her limits, and if she does too much in one day it can set off an episode, either high, or low. If something excites my mum, I worry she's going to get mania, or if something upsets her, I worry she is going to become depressed. I'll often say to my mum, 'Is this going to make you ill?' as I need the reassurance that she is OK.

I've learnt to know that I have to talk about my mum's bipolar if I'm upset, in order to feel better, but I don't feel comfortable talking about her being unwell as I feel as if I'm being a pain.

I worry about my sister when my mum's unwell and we do talk about it sometimes, and reassuring her that everything is going to be fine helps me know that as well. My sister is lucky as she has close friends she can and will talk to which makes me feel better knowing she can do that.

There's no one I can say is more of a role model than my mum. She is constantly fighting bipolar to keep on top of everything and stay well. She has proved to both me and Tasha what a real mum should be like, and by managing everyday things, whilst writing a book and fighting bipolar, she always wins, and nothing gets in the way of that.

I'm so proud to say Cara Aiken is my mum. My mum's the best mum in the world.

Tasha Aiken, 15 years old

I'm not too sure how old my mum was when she first got bipolar but I know that I grew up with it. The first time I really remember her having an episode was when I was about six or seven, and I remember being out, and my dad telling me to come home. My mum was sitting there because she had been in hospital for six weeks and it was so nice just to see her.

When my mum is high, I feel very weird and controlling, but I don't like that because I can't control her. When she is low I do feel like *her* mum and I really don't like it because it does upset me, and people say I need to understand her illness even though I do, but people don't understand that it does still upset me however much I understand her.

I sometimes feel that I want to just have bipolar for just a minute, just to see what my mum is going through, but I wouldn't always want it because I know it is a hard and stressful illness.

At the moment I feel like she is always ill even on the days she feels fine, only because it has been going on for such a long time, but I can definitely see that she is better on some days because she is a completely different person. My mum has been getting mania more than being depressed it seems at the moment. When my mum is depressed or manic, to be honest, I don't want to be around her, but when she is depressed I never know what to do, I don't know whether she wants people to comfort her or if she wants to be on her own. When my mum has mania that's even worse because I only feel safe when she is in bed because I know that nothing can happen.

In my old house when furniture was moved round and when the house was always clean and catalogues were out, that's when I knew she had mania. It is a hard thing as a child to completely understand everything, however well it is explained, and some people expect me to understand it all.

The bipolar controls my mum and she does not control the bipolar because if she controlled it then she would stop it, although some medication helps. But the medication that helps her, makes her go to sleep or does something different to her which isn't good.

My mum makes a lot of arrangements but usually cancels them because she does not feel well enough to see her friends. None of her friends get angry with her because all her friends know about her illness and all she has to say is that she doesn't feel good today and they are fine with that.

When my mum gets mania, the thing that triggers it off is if she 'overdoes it' which means if she does too much in one day, or she does the cleaning and then gets a bit 'high'. Also going into big crowds and shopping centres, or even if she is in a rush to leave the house if she has somewhere to be this triggers mania. I don't think there is anything that triggers her depression unless something bad happens and she gets upset about it.

Her bipolar has not affected any friendships and the support she gets from friends and family is very good.

When she is really ill, I don't usually talk to friends because they all say the same thing saying, 'Aww, I hope she gets better.' They don't understand as much as some people and they also say they know how it feels which annoys me because they really don't because none of their mums are ill like mine. Most of my friends just think it is like a broken leg or arm and it will heal, and they don't understand that it won't.

I used to have a counsellor in my old school and I found her very helpful, but then I moved school. I talk to my auntie or my dad a lot if it is upsetting me. When my mum gave me a lot of information about bipolar I found it helpful and it made me understand a lot better and she explained that she isn't as bad as ever committing suicide or anything as bad as that, but I have seen the worst of her. I sometimes talk to my sister because I find that helpful because we are both in exactly the same position. I know she has found things very hard and I want her to talk to me even if I can't help, because I am out with her a lot and I want her to be able to tell me anything.

When Mummy is ill, especially with depression, I definitely can see a change because she wears no make-up at all and she usually has puffy eyes from crying and she is usually tired when she is ill. She usually stays in her pyjamas or dressing gown so that she is comfortable and not cold. It is a big difference though.

Mummy might be going to a special hospital which really should help her, and make her episodes happen after a much longer time. People that I have spoken to have taught me not to think she is going to get better permanently but I have been taught to think that it won't get any worse than I have ever seen her before.

Growing up with a bipolar parent: Sharon's children

Sharon has written her account of parenting with bipolar disorder in Chapter 3. When she asked her children, Hannah and Jack, whether they would be willing to write something for my book, she wrote me a message under their contributions. It says, 'I'm shocked. My son Jack has never mentioned his feelings before. Thanks to you, I got the above.' I am hoping that all the parents and their children who are involved in my project will have developed a better understanding of each other's feelings.

Hannah, 12 years old

I was about six or seven years old when I realized my mum had bipolar. I think she was ill before that because she was always crying and going to bed during the daytime to rest.

I do see my mum active sometimes, always running around after me and my brother, and I wonder how she does it. I don't always think of my mum being ill. I see my mum as both being well and unwell. But when she is being active, I don't even think about her being ill. Mum suffers from more of the depressive side, where she just cries and goes up to bed to sleep. I feel bored and lonely at these times. I want to understand but I just can't get my head around it. Sometimes I don't know what I can do to help.

Mum often gets all worried if we are invited to parties, as she knows there will be a lot of people there, so she often can't manage to go. Also, if she plans something and then ends up having an episode, she will probably ask me to cancel that plan and we will stay at home.

Sometimes I feel more like my mum's parent because, at times, I have to look after her and my brother. I have to make tea and things like that.

Mum's bipolar hasn't actually affected any of my friendships, but I can only bring friends home sometimes.

I do worry a bit about developing bipolar myself because I wouldn't want to be crying all the time, and it seems as if my mum is always tired. I want to be active.

Being the older child makes life a bit harder when your mum suffers from bipolar. Sometimes you can feel stuck in the dark, because other children are playing out and we can't because Mum is in bed, so we are inside bored.

I have to do lots of jobs to help and it gets on my nerves and then I get upset and shout at Mum which then makes her far worse. Life is hard but we do have good times when Mum is well.

I have support from a young carers group. I also have the same friends and family as my mum, and they all say I can talk to them if I'm worried and I do. Also I talk to her nurse. I have a little brother who is 16 months younger than me, but I don't feel able to talk to him about Mum's illness.

Jack, 11 years old

> I feel like I have run around the world a thousand times because me and my sister have to help my mum because she is poorly sometimes. She gets very tired. I feel so sad at times but I am a person who tries to keep my feelings inside.

Growing up with a bipolar parent: Tracey's children

When I approached Tracey with regard to her children David, James and Bethan writing a little something from their viewpoint, only David was willing to contribute. She was very surprised to learn that her bipolar disorder hadn't had much of an impact on her son, and she felt very complimented by his entry. A year later, Tracey approached me as to whether I would still be interested in having James' and Bethan's accounts. I was delighted to read them.

All three of her children, none of whom was particularly affected by her illness, have developed a good understanding of bipolar disorder, and maintain a very positive attitude, not only to the illness, but towards their mother too. Tracey has written her account of parenting with bipolar in Chapter 3.

All three of Tracey's children have been brought up with strong religious beliefs. Their faith has taught them to think so positively about her bipolar disorder, which is truly reflected in their personal accounts.

David, 20 years old

> I had a very happy childhood, and didn't think my life had any problems at all. This was probably because my parents hid troubles from me and I was being non-observant of things around me. I slowly began to realize that things around me weren't quite normal when I was about eight or nine when we moved house and country. We moved to a cul-de-sac with lots of kids around the place. I slowly began to realize that everyone else's mums were always up, and always busy. Whereas my mum spent a lot of the time in bed, with what I was led to believe were migraines and at the time I just

assumed that was the case. I have a lot of memories of Mum being up and about but also a lot of her being in bed snoring the whole house out!

I don't remember Mum having bipolar ever affecting my friendships, as she was fine in letting me bring friends round to play on the Playstation, etc. But I do remember her embarrassing me by pretending to be a gorilla when coming to collect me from outside where I was playing with the 'cool' boys and me being very embarrassed and not seeing the funny side of it.

Having a parent with bipolar I feel that I have matured a lot more quickly than I was supposed to. But I'm not complaining as I am happy with who I am. I feel that there are times when I help Mum out, by telling her she's going too high, that she needs to calm down and go to bed or just a hug and a kiss when she's feeling low. I'm not my mother's carer as she is a very 'high functioning' sufferer of bipolar. She's a great mother to me. The caring role goes both ways. I will look after her if she is ill and she looks after me as her son. I guess in a way I just see my mum as a very good friend rather than a mother sometimes.

I don't have a fear of bipolar as I don't feel the need to fear something if there's nothing you can do about it. As long as I can have a fulfilling and enjoyable life then I'm perfectly happy. As I said earlier I see my mum as a high functioning mother. I try not to focus on the memories of her being ill but on the happy memories of my mum just being my mum. So I guess subconsciously I've blocked out a lot of the memories of Mum being ill.

My mum in general is very well in my opinion though she does have a varied mix of manic and depressive episodes. It used to be a lot worse. I have a distinct memory of Mum buying pretty much everything in every catalogue for Christmas. But with recent therapy and change of drugs she's been able to stop the highs very well on her own. With the depressive states she is getting better at controlling them, but it is still very hard now and again for me to understand that she just wants to lie in bed.

Episodes don't usually affect me too greatly as I've become used to them. I don't take it on my own shoulders to 'fix Mum'. But when she does have an episode either way, I just do my part around the house, whether it's cook for the kids or tidy up the lounge. I usually just do what I can rather than take on impossible tasks.

Well, my mum has been fighting the bipolar and succeeding very well in the last year or so. I feel the bipolar did used to control her but as she's been learning more about it and going to therapy she's able to fight it and live a more 'normal' functioning life. I have a lot of admiration for my mum doing this.

I'm not completely sure what medical care she does have, as I know she's had a lot of problems, and a lot of them don't even involve bipolar, but I do know she goes and sees a psychiatrist solely for her bipolar, which I know has been a great help to her. Also Mum spent about two months in hospital for her depression, and got herself sorted even though it was hell for her living in the mental institution. I know that she didn't do it for herself but for the family.

I don't have any formal support like care workers or anything like that as I don't feel it necessary. My parents understand that I sometimes need to get out and go and chill at a mate's house. So for support I have my family and friends and that's all I need.

From what I know triggers usually involve death as it reminds Mum of her mother's death and that usually sends her into a downward spiral. Also misunderstandings in the family and conflict in general trigger her to have a depressive episode. But as I said before she's getting better in the last year or so and she can control these episodes a lot better.

Triggers for becoming manic are usually over-stimulation when she has had a really action-packed day or has got too excited about something. These usually start her off on a manic episode.

Mum's episodes are rarer now as far as I know, as we as a family and her on her own are getting better at identifying the beginning stages of these episodes. If I had to put a figure on it I would say it's one every two to three months. Maybe even less than that. Mum always has us as family; she has some really good friends in the church, not so many out of it as a lot of them have just grown distant over time. She also has religion which above all things helps her get through it.

As I have an autistic brother and a young sister it's not something we usually talk about. But sometimes I say to my little sister, 'Mum is not well and don't disturb her' but apart from that I feel that seeing as they are a lot younger I don't feel the need to talk to them about anything deep as I wouldn't want to burden them with problems they can't solve.

James, 15 years old

I wasn't always aware that my mum had bipolar disorder. I first noticed when she had to go into hospital a lot when I was about 11 years old. I didn't know why she was in hospital until it was explained to me. After that, even though I knew she had bipolar, I didn't really think much of it until my brother, David, left home, because he was five years older than me, and he took the brunt of it. That meant I didn't have to, but when he left home two years ago, the torch was passed down to me.

Over the past year, I have found myself taking charge of situations when my mum is either going high or low. I had to come home early from school last week, to look after her, as she was very down, and could not be left on her own. My dad was at work and her close friends were all out. That had never happened before. I cuddled her and listened to her while she cried. I gave her some reassurance that she said really helped her. Straight after I had finished comforting her, my big brother David phoned, and reassured her as well. He prayed with her over the phone which she said really helped. We were like a little team, pulling together. Even my sister Beth was at home, as she had just had her tonsils out. So we all pulled together.

I can't really say her illness has affected me, because I don't know any different. I guess it has helped mould me into the person I am today, along with my Christian faith. Without it, I wouldn't be who I am.

I could say that, at times, it has made my social life a drag, as Mum has not always been well enough to take me out, or have friends round. I can't blame it all on my mum, because I have Asperger's syndrome, which is high-function autism, and I kind of like to be by myself, with my computer games anyway. I would say that life with a bipolar parent has reassured me, as it has made me stronger than others, in the way I can take charge in difficult situations. My mum and I share a really silly sense of humour together, and when one of us gets laughing, it sets the other one off. And we just can't stop! We dare not look at each other sometimes, and we don't even know why we are laughing!

My mum often apologizes for being a bad mum when she is down, and I have had to help her, but I just tell her she is the best mother I could wish for. And then she starts crying all over again!

Bethan, 9 years old

When Mummy is ill and crying, I hug her and kiss her and bring her a toilet roll to wipe her eyes and to blow her nose on. I tell her not to worry what other people think, because God made her the way she is, and he loves her so she shouldn't worry what other people say.

Last week she was really sad, and I was home from school because I had just had my tonsils out. I hugged her, kissed her and then went and rang my dad at work. He was in a meeting, so I left him a message to ring back, because Mummy was poorly. He gave me some extra pocket money for doing that, and I bought some guns to go with my cowgirl outfit.

I don't remember Mummy being in hospital as I was too little. If Mummy is sad, she often goes upstairs to her room to have a rest, and if there is nobody else in the house with us, I get scared on my own downstairs, in case someone breaks in and steals me away. When I am sick, my mummy cuddles and kisses me and pinches my bottom, because she says it is soft like two peaches in a hanky. When she says she is sorry because she is not a very good mum, I say I think you are brilliant and the best mum I could ever have.

I would be lost without her even though the bipolar makes her sad sometimes. I need her to look after me, and she teaches me how to sew, make things out of papier mâché, and paint. I don't want her to change. When she is sad, she cries a lot, blows her nose and her face goes bright red, which is funny. I like it better when she is sad and I can cuddle and kiss her, because when she is busy, she does lots of chores that don't need doing, and I can't cuddle her and make her feel better. When she is busy, she does not spend so much time with me. Sometimes she embarrasses me by telling my friends silly stories about when I was little.

I love my mum the whole world and back times a million.

Growing up with a bipolar parent: the experiences of adult children

It is easy to forget that we do not cease to be someone's child when we reach the age of 21. In this section, I have collected the experiences of adult children of parents living with bipolar disorder.

Growing up with a bipolar parent: Debbie

Debbie writes about her father who took his own life after developing bipolar disorder at the age of 60.

My beloved dad died on 24 May 2003, but to me he died a long time before that. In November 1999 he went to his holiday home in Florida with my mum... I always say that he never came back again.

When I think back to the months leading up to that date, there were definite indications that he was undergoing a huge personality change. My dad was my absolute hero, a successful business man, a perfectionist in every way, a loving family man, who was passionate about life and could handle anything that life threw at him.

He turned 60 in September 1999 and I, his middle daughter, noticed that things did not seem quite right. He began to be more agitated, more irritable, minor ailments started really bothering him that would never have bothered him before and he seemed so sad all the time.

My mum had noticed similar behaviour changes but thought that a trip to their holiday home in Florida would change how he was feeling – in fact it had the opposite effect. Evidently immediately upon arriving, he had immense difficulty sleeping. This was not the normal jet lag; he was suffering from nearly complete sleep deprivation.

His best friend, John, and his wife, Mary, were staying with my parents in Florida and John told me at a later date that my dad said to him that if he did not take him back home immediately, he was scared he was going to die out there...they came home a week early. I saw him the next day and nothing could have prepared me. Gone was my strong, powerful dad, and in his place was a shaky, frightened man with staring eyes...

John took him immediately to see their private doctor who diagnosed a form of breakdown and prescribed sedatives. I think that at the time he did indicate to John that this was not an illness that would disappear in a few days. Up to this point the word 'depression' was not mentioned.

The following months leading up to Christmas were filled with doctor's appointments – he had at the time a very sympathetic doctor (GP) who I believe prescribed sleeping tablets and antidepressants. I and my two sisters were to a degree kept in the dark about the kind of medication he was on and there was a kind of taboo about the whole subject.

As siblings we handled it quite differently. My younger sister did not want anyone to know that he was 'unwell', and my older sister blamed the fact that Dad had no hobbies! He had recently taken a step back in his business and was almost working on a consultancy basis. I, however, began looking up depression on the internet and reading as much literature as possible on the subject.

Just before the New Year he seemed to make a full recovery and the whole family were thrilled. He seemed almost to come back to us again as the man we remembered but somehow there was always this sense of foreboding that one day this terrible illness would return... It did and this time it was much worse.

What followed then were episodes which seemed to grow closer and closer in time. He suffered a couple of manic attacks when he decided to sell his house, buy a new house, spend an absolute fortune on furnishings, etc., order a new car... but the deep depressions dominated most of the episodes. I found it so hard to comprehend how quickly these episodes could happen. I could see him one day, laughing and joking and absolutely fine – then the next morning I would go round to see him and he would answer the door with the vacant, glazed look in his eyes that I began to recognize and in time dread.

Until you have seen someone with actual real depression you cannot even begin to comprehend it – it is like the soul has been sucked out of them and all that is left is a shell with staring eyes. My mum and I always say there could not have been a more torturous illness for my dad to get. His confidence went, his sparkle went, his whole personality changed.

He hated the drugs he was on, hated how they made him feel. A spell in the Priory in 2002 to me was a complete and utter waste of time and every time we visited him I felt like I had betrayed him by leaving him there as he used to beg us over and over again not to leave him.

During this time I felt such utter desolation and despair – not only did I feel like I had lost my dad, but also I was worried sick about my mum who seemed to be at her wits' end. My two young sons who were nine and 12 at the time were also deeply affected as their loving 'dida' whom they were used to seeing on an almost daily basis was kept away from them.

His doctor (GP) whom he had seemed to build some sort of rapport with left the practice and from then on he began to see a number of psychiatrists privately – none of whom he felt completely relaxed with, none of whom he trusted. I went along to a number of appointments with him and it was at one of these appointments that I first heard the word 'bipolar'. I had already read up on the condition and identified most of the symptoms as what my dad was suffering. When I think back to these appointments I realize now that my dad never seemed to really 'open up' during them.

His medication was changed a number of times and he still had huge difficulty sleeping. He also started going down the pub a lot with his brother and group of friends, something he had never done before.

Every Monday night my mum would go to play bridge and when my dad was suffering one of his depressions he would come over to me for dinner. I was living with my two sons and my younger sister was living with me on a temporary basis. We dreaded those evenings to some degree – not because we did not want to see our dad but because for the first hour it was so, so difficult. He would go over and over the same things, how he felt so low, so tired, hated how the drugs were making him feel, and we would try to cheer him and talk to him. Towards the end of the evening though the depression did lift slightly.

During his depressions he seemed to turn to me more and more. Anyone who has actually lived with someone with bipolar as was the case with my mum will know that it has got to be one of the hardest things to deal with – and at certain stages your patience to a degree does run out. I am not criticizing my mum at all, she was always there for him, always cared for him but there were times when I could see it was getting to her and then she would snap at him. She says now nearly five years after he died that she would give anything in the world to have him back again and I know she means it. Maybe the fact that I was not actually living with him meant I had more patience. I would listen to him for hours, comfort him, try to console him and I used to promise him that he would get better. On a few occasions he just appeared at my house, looking so forlorn and frightened it almost broke my heart seeing him like that.

From the research I carried out I knew that actually there was no cure – I was just hoping that one day they would find a drug that could stabilize my dad's episodes and let him have a certain quality of life. However this was not to be the case.

During the early hours of 24 May 2003 – the day of my younger son's tenth birthday party – my dad took his own life. The weeks that followed were probably the most heartbreaking days that I will ever experience. 'Why did he do it?' was the question asked over and over again. How could he do it to his wife, his girls, his grandchildren, his best friend, his brother? The list goes on and on – a suicide has a huge ripple effect and reaches out to many people. I however can to a degree understand why he did it – to live in a world where there is no light, but just darkness, to live in a world full of utter despair and pain – to be so tortured day after day – that's the life my lovely, strong, incredibly brave dad had…and that is why I don't feel anyone has the right to ask why he did it. All I know is that for nearly 37 years I had the most wonderful dad and I am so proud of the type of man he was and of everything he stood for – as a family we are in some ways continuing to pick up the pieces of what his suicide did. I am not angry with my dad but I am in some ways angry with the medical system as I do feel it let him down to some degree.

I am however determined that this trauma in my life will not destroy me nor my children, that we shall all somehow learn from it, and appreciate that nothing in life is guaranteed.

I pray that some day there will be some kind of medical breakthrough and that there will be an actual cure for this terrible condition that I can only describe as a living hell.

Growing up with a bipolar parent: anonymous

This lady wishes to remain anonymous, but I feel the need to include her account of her childhood experience of her bipolar father which has had a profound effect on her as an adult. She has not been haunted by the fear that she might have inherited the illness, but she has had a strong desire to walk away from her feelings and not confront them.

I remember waking up in the night, at times, aware that he was pacing around downstairs, unable to sleep. Or he would wake painfully early in the morning and be sitting at his typewriter full of ideas. Later in the day, he would insist my mother listen while he read out what great things he had written. I didn't understand the content much, but I could tell it was often embarrassing and over the top.

On more than one occasion, I recall sitting at the supper table and him appearing at the front door, earlier than usual, having been given the sack. He reported what the argument had been about with his boss. We all sensed that he had been extreme with the boss, but he wouldn't hear any criticism. He was the only one with insight, after all. My mother's heart would sink – we could see it on her face and felt we'd better not say anything.

There was crying and despair. He would waste money – he never had any. My brother and I wondered why, when there was something to be paid for at school, all the other children had a cheque from their parents' joint bank account and we had one from our mother's separate bank account (she worked), never from my dad. My brother and I became grown up and sensible rather early because we sensed that actually, far from Dad looking after us, we had to look after him. I became middle aged before my time.

I've taken a very long time to settle down and have a child – well into my forties and none of it was planned. My brother was late too. I think there are two reasons for this. I previously never particularly wanted to have children or be settled in a marriage like my mother's situation, in case I couldn't escape, because my assumption was it would be painful. I wanted my freedom.

I also wanted to be alone, not to have to live day-by-day alert on the look out for the behaviour of someone to change and be frightened of it. It was too nerve-racking. I didn't want to put the stress and pain onto myself again or onto anyone else, certainly not a child. I didn't want the responsibility of others on my shoulders. I didn't like it when I was a child. After my dad died, I spent many years abroad, just enjoying not being burdened with the weight and worry I grew up with. I could just be me. I was happy.

I also feel that I have never been sure if I am OK or not, as a person. I am professionally successful and have many wonderful close friends and now a lovely partner and child. But, when the person who loved me above all else (my dad) had so many episodes of clearly absurd behaviour and thinking, it's as though I can't trust his opinion in loving me: his endorsement of me can't have been reliable.

As a result, I've spent much of my life longing to be really ordinary.[4]

Growing up with a bipolar parent: Sandy Knox

Sandy, who herself has bipolar disorder, grew up with a bipolar mother.

I didn't know my mother was ill or suffering. I only know how I felt. I felt disappointed and frustrated which manifested into fear and anxiety. It's the inconsistency that gets to you. The never knowing what you'll find when you get home

4 This text originally appeared as an article in the Winter 2006 edition of *Pendulum.*

from school. On a really good day there would be music playing or the TV on or both. She'd have her pinny on, standing at the sink peeling potatoes or scraping carrots. She might have been baking and you'd smell the sweetness of pastry and sponge cakes in the air. Oh, happy days.

On a bad day the house would be cold, silent. She'd be asleep on the settee, pinny on, paper hanky stuffed in her hand, swollen eyes. Oh, the disappointment. I'd just stand there looking at her, not understanding, and not knowing she was ill. The cold silence of the house was oppressive. 'Mam,' I'd whisper, 'Mam, are you going to wake up now?' 'Just five more minutes, I've only just lain down,' she'd slur.

My fears and anxieties grew as I grew because I didn't quite trust her with things that I thought were important. And let's face it, when you're a kid everything to do with you is important. For example, if I had to bring something to school like a costume for a play, a packed lunch or a letter, I did not feel confident that she wouldn't let me down.

When I was about eight years old, we had a Christmas party at school. Everyone was to bring his or her own party packed lunch. I had given my mam plenty of notice and told her exactly what I'd like in my party lunch box. I so wanted to be just like the other girls, especially to have my own beaker with a snap-on lid. I was so excited about the party yet full of dread and panic that it would all go wrong. I went to sleep worrying about it, I awoke worrying about it.

On the morning of the party I reminded my mam again as she lay in bed comatose.

'Mam, Mam,' I spoke quietly. 'Mam, you won't forget my party packed lunch, will you?' 'No, I won't,' she mumbled. School that morning was overshadowed by worry so I learned very little that day. I usually went home for lunch, skipping all the way and today was no exception. She was up and well and there was someone else in the house, an auntie maybe, so she didn't have much time for me.

She had made me a chocolate cake. A square chocolate cake with butter cream icing. That was my party lunch.

'Mam, no, I have to take a proper lunch with sandwiches and cakes and a beaker of juice.' I was frantic.

'No, you don't, everyone takes one thing and the teachers share it all out.'

'No, Mam, not this time, we have to have, the teacher said, we have to have…'

I cried all the way to school with my chocolate cake. I didn't want to go because I thought everyone would laugh at me. And they did. Even the teachers. Mrs Nendick offered to ask the other kids if they'd do a swap with me, but I insisted I wanted that cake, that I loved it and had meant to bring it. All around me the other kids were eating their triangle sandwiches and chocolate mini rolls out of their lovely Tupperware boxes and sipping squash out of their beakers with the snap-on lids.

I had my solitary, dry chocolate cake and a cup of water given to me by the teacher. I ate as much as I could with tears in my eyes, but it was hard to get it past the lump in my throat. That's probably the first time I began to have feelings of hatred for my mam because I trusted her and she let me down because she never listened.

As I got older and hit my teen years, she was becoming a moody, bitter nag and I'm ashamed to say that I hated her. I thought she was pathetic. She was often in bed or lying on the settee or crying. She didn't pay me much attention and there was a period of quite a few years when she didn't seem to care about me. That was partly good because it meant she wasn't on my back, but it also meant I didn't have any support and I was going through a hell of my own with depression. My father would give me a good 'finger-in-the-face' talking to. His bottom line was, 'Snap out of it or I'll knock it out of you.' Nice.

It's the inconsistency that gets to you the most. If she were consistently down or consistently high, it would have been easier. Like my dad – he was difficult to live with but at least I knew where I stood with him because he was consistently grumpy and sullen. Not knowing what to expect when you walk or skip through the front door – happy or sad, warm or cold – makes you anxious and fearful.

My mam's illness affected everyone in the household. It was not a pleasant home a lot of the time. My dad called her a stupid bloody woman, always snivelling. They argued every night in the kitchen, doors closed, before he left for his night shift. My brother, who also suffers depression, treated her with disdain, and my sister, also a manic depressive, treated her a little better. All in all, my mother lived in a home where nobody was nice to her, put down at every turn. Life was really hard for her yet she always, always put a good meal on the table. I just don't know how she did it.

After successfully hiding my depression for many years, I finally succumbed to an almighty breakdown and found myself, like my mother, hiding from the reality of hopelessness by taking to my bed. Only now do I understand what I couldn't understand as a child and my mother is forgiven and forgives.

But what of my own son, what is his mother's bipolar disorder doing to him?

Growing up with a bipolar parent: Koulla Zavros

Koulla is the daughter of a bipolar mother. She lives in Hertfordshire, England, with her husband and two sons. Koulla is Greek. Her mother lives in Cyprus but makes regular visits to England to see Koulla and her family. Koulla doesn't appear in any other chapters, but I felt very strongly about including her experience of growing up with a bipolar mother.

Life was pretty normal; we had a good family life. Mum was loving, caring, and always did a lot with us. She was a very attractive lady and always took pride in herself and her appearance.

I don't know what went wrong or why, but in the summer of 1986, my brothers and I lost our mum, and Dad lost his wife. My brother Lazarus was 22, I was 18, and my youngest brother Mario was just seven. Dad rang me to go to my aunt's because Mum was very ill. We called a doctor and my mother had her first breakdown at the age of 45.

After this episode, mum had relapse after relapse, and finally our doctor referred Mum to the hospital where she was diagnosed with bipolar disorder. It was all totally new to us, we had never heard the word 'bipolar', and neither did we know what it meant. We had never known anyone with this illness. I was frightened because Mum's behaviour had changed. She felt very low in mood and felt as if there was nothing to live for. She suffered psychosis, delusions, paranoia and cried a lot. Mum got extremely low. She had stopped eating properly, was always in bed, stayed in the same clothes for days on end, and it became an effort for her to wash.

My life changed too. I became my mother's mother. I had to take care of my little brother, help my dad, cook and do all the household chores. I would also have to encourage Mum to have a bath, change her clothes and eat.

It hurt to see Mum in this way. I would hold back the tears and put on a brave face as I didn't want my little brother to worry, and Mum to see me in this way. I would go to bed and cry and hold my cross and pray that when I woke up in the morning, Mum would be her normal self. I would worry about Dad and my little brother. The only way to stay strong was to take one day at a time.

How did my brother Mario feel? Well, even though he knows Mum, he feels like he's never had a mum. He never had a normal childhood from the age of seven. He never had friends round, nor went round to friends. Mum was very over-protective towards him. When Mario was at primary school, mum had a manic episode and she decided to squat in the headmaster's office. Mario wasn't aware of this as he was in class. Police were called, also Mum's doctor and Dad. Mum had to be escorted off the premises and taken away in an ambulance to the hospital. She was sectioned, and had to stay in hospital for four weeks. This was very upsetting for the whole family. We felt so hurt, and it was out of our control. Mum couldn't control her actions and behaviour.

Even when Mario was at secondary school, Mum would wait for him at the gate. She would walk him to school and walk him home. Mario began to hate school; he became very shy and lost all his confidence. He never really spoke of Mum's illness to his friends. He became dependent on me and my older brother Lazarus. Mario also missed a lot of school because of Mum's illness.

My poor dad had to split himself into three. He had to work to support us, run the house, do the shopping, cook, and care for Mum. We would cook a meal for Mum and take it to the hospital every evening for four weeks. I would help bath Mum, dress her and encourage her to eat. We wanted to build her self-esteem up and get her back to her normal self.

Dad took Mum and Mario to Cyprus, and they stayed there for four or five months. He thought it would do Mum some good, but she really missed us and wanted to come home. Mario's school work suffered, especially his reading and writing.

Many of our childhood and teenage memories are of Mum in the mental unit as she was sectioned many times after this first episode.

What upsets me the most is that since Mum was diagnosed until today's date, we have never had any professional support or counselling. Also, back in 1986, there was very limited information about bipolar disorder. We went through this illness with Mum in complete darkness. It is only now, in our adulthood, that we have grown to understand this illness.

Do I fear developing bipolar disorder myself? Yes, I do have this fear and am sure my brothers share the same feelings. If I'm ever feeling low, I make sure I pick myself up; I change any negative thoughts to positive ones. I share my feelings or worries and speak to my close friends or immediate family.

As Mum has got older, she has been suffering with more of the manic symptoms as opposed to depression. Her behaviour varies when in mania. We tend to know the signs now. She may dress outrageously; she's very excited, feels on top of the world and speaks very quickly. She is sometimes verbally abusive and disturbs the public. Her behaviour is spontaneous.

Once, Mum got up and took my dad's credit card and went on a spending spree. She decided to buy a violin even though she didn't have a clue how to play it. Other times Mum would go into the town dressed up as if she was going to a wedding, and sometimes make rude hand gestures to people she didn't like. Dad would sometimes get calls from the police station telling him what Mum had done. We didn't know, but the police had a big file of Mum's incidents. They quite understood as they know about Mum's illness. When Mum got very bad, she would have to be sectioned.

I definitely think that the bipolar controls my mum's life. Due to the bipolar bringing on paranoia and psychosis, Mum thinks that what's in her mind is actually happening to her and therefore she feels that bad things will happen to her or people dislike her. She stays home more and more as she feels safe. She doesn't go out shopping or socializing.

Mum has lost all her confidence; she finds it very hard to manage her day-to-day responsibilities. My dad tends to manage the food shopping, work and general running of the house. Mum will cook, but sometimes needs encouragement from Dad. She manages a little house work. Many times she'll ring me to say that she can't get motivated and loses concentration. She doesn't know where to start with her daily chores. We have suggested many hobbies for her to start that she used to enjoy, but she's very negative and has no interest.

Does something trigger off Mum's mania or depression? Well, we're always guessing. Sometimes we think that Mum finds it really difficult to deal with any problems or tragic news – whether it's a family problem or something she's heard on the news. I think Mum's ideal world would be that everyone is happy, safe, healthy and kind to each other.

Mum's episodes may only be one in two years now, but when she has an episode, it lasts a lot longer and has got worse each time. Dad makes sure now that she visits a psychiatrist regularly, normally once a month. They monitor her closely and make sure she is on the right medication.

Mum's always had our support, but now she is in Cyprus and so dad is her main support. Mum has four siblings, but because of the way she has behaved sometimes, I think they keep their distance. Mum has insulted them or their children in the past. I don't think that they are very well informed, or have any knowledge about bipolar. Therefore they get offended. Some people who live in Mum's village just think she is a mad woman. It's a vicious circle because family and friends avoid Mum, so as not to upset her, but then Mum feels rejected and disowned. This makes her feel more paranoid and unwanted.

Mum really loves her grandchildren more than anything in the world. She is very over-protective and rings regularly from Cyprus to talk to them. She has had a manic episode in front of the children, which was very upsetting for them. They have experienced her screaming, her unusual behaviour and her breaking down in tears. My brother and I have sat them down and explained their Nanny's illness to them. When they were young, it was just Nanny not feeling very well, but once they were old enough to understand, we explained what bipolar was. The older grandchildren have taken a big interest and read up on the illness.

Even though Dad has been very strong through all this, it has affected him immensely. Mum has been totally dependent on Dad. His social life became non-existent for many years. It is a little better now that he is in Cyprus, as he spends time in his orchard and sometimes goes to the café to meet friends. But he is still near Mum as the village is small. Also, now that he has retired, he spends a lot more time with her.

I would like to think that there is hope for the future for my mum and other people suffering with mental illness. I hope and wish that with more funding and medical research into mental health, help for sufferers will progress. I don't believe that Mum will ever get over her bipolar, but with plenty of knowledge, information and close monitoring, counselling and new medical research, we may together be able to control the bipolar rather than the bipolar controlling the victim.

Growing up with a bipolar parent: Michel

The following is Michel's story as recounted by Cara. Michel's story describes him caring for his bipolar father and developing bipolar disorder himself.

Prior to Michel's first breakdown in 1991 and a subsequent suicide attempt, he had a professional background as a journalist, initially working as a management writer and Careers Editor for *The Times*. He also combined freelance work as a journalist with academic work as a researcher and lecturer. In the late 1980s, he was a visiting Fellow at Cranfield School of Management and also at the University of Hong Kong where he worked for six years during the 1990s.

Michel feels his suicide attempt was a 'cry for help' as he was in total despair at the thought of inheriting manic depression, the same illness which his father had developed in 1965, and whose life it had destroyed.

Although Michel's father was running extremely 'high' for approximately ten years preceding his diagnosis, with eccentric, excitable, over-energetic and very destructive behaviour, the family had not realized he was extremely ill. He had also become promiscuous, and hugely over-spent.

Prior to his father's diagnosis in 1965, the family were extremely 'well off', upper-middle-class citizens who lived in a lovely home. Due to his behaviour and in particular the constant spending, over a period of time, his father became bankrupt and had to move his family to a flat.

Michel only realized the seriousness of his father's illness when he was taken out of boarding school at the age of 11. Michel says, 'Manic depression may have impaired my life, but it completely ruined his. His career and business were entirely destroyed and his marriage to my mother was put under enormous strain.' They eventually divorced to protect his mother's life, although they maintained close contact until he died.

Michel took over the role as his father's primary carer during his late teens and early twenties. He says, 'In the rather primitive conditions that existed then, "care" usually meant forcing him into hospital under the provisions of the Mental Health Act.' He was directly involved in placing him under a section 12 times. This put their relationship under a great deal of stress. During these years, gradually, Michel took on a parental role to his own father and became an authority figure to him. As a result, his father started acting like a naughty child towards Michel which wasn't a very healthy relationship for either of them.

Despite Michel's father's illness and predominantly his mania, he set up a public relations company and managed, alongside his son, to become a very early member of the Manic Depression Fellowship.[5] Together, they played significant roles in the charity – they helped with the founding of it, and Michel became its second Chair. When Michel was 27, and his father was 64, they both took part in a television programme called *The Claire Rayner Casebook* (Channel 4, 2006) which had a huge impact on the charity (as did the more recent documentary involving Stephen Fry: *The Secret Life of the Manic Depressive* (BBC, September 2008)). Their membership trebled overnight.

Michel's father enjoyed a relative level of stability during the last five years of his life due to the social services stepping in. They funded adult foster care for him that offered ongoing continuity so that he always had a home to return to after a hospital admission.

In 1997 Michel suffered a further breakdown which led to his diagnosis of manic depression. Michel feels that he displayed symptoms of this illness for at least a decade

5   This organization is now known as MDF The Bipolar Organization.

before this. He had a high-flying career which was extremely pressurized and he travelled and worked internationally. In the wake of his breakdown and diagnosis, Michel reconciled himself to giving up his very successful but stressful career. He totally down-sized his life and income – in fact his income was reduced by 75 per cent if not more. From 1997 to approximately 2004, Michel found it impossible to sustain work contracts (although getting them was easy), and had to pull out through these years.

When I met Michel in October 2007, I asked him how he manages his current responsibilities and how he copes with pressure. He answered, 'I have a better feel for what I can cope with, I'm open with my work clients, and would back out of work to put my health first. I'm realistic about what I can and cannot cope with and have to balance my work commitments.' Whenever possible, he takes a rest or sleeps for an hour or so each afternoon.

When asked if bipolar disorder controls his life, or if he controls the bipolar, he told me that he definitely controls his bipolar. He says, 'If you had asked me that a year ago, I would most certainly have said the bipolar controlled me.' Michel has a very good support network in his friends and his community psychiatric nurse (CPN). But most importantly he has a bipolar partner whom he is marrying next year. They most certainly complement each other and their relationship is a wonderful stabilizer for them both – they recognize each other's early symptoms, and his partner's parents not only support their daughter, but have also fully extended their support to Michel. Michel now lives in Scotland – he married his finances with his mother's, has no mortgage to worry about, and life has become much less stressful.

The only issue that still lives on in Michel is the legacy of heavy guilt regarding his father's illness. 'Particularly after my breakdown in 1997, I did feel increasingly guilty and uncomfortable about how supportive our relationship actually had been. I moved in my own mind from seeing manic depression through the eyes of someone who was a carer, to someone who actually suffers directly from the illness. I could see the pain but couldn't feel what it was like.' Michel feels he should have been more affectionate and loving towards his father rather than just treating him and his condition as 'something to be managed'. He has a distinct memory of turning up at the hospital on one occasion and finding his father crying, with a look of complete despair on his face.

This has left Michel with a legacy of heavy guilt and a huge unresolved question: who is to blame? No one is to blame. Was his father the benign child, or was it the illness that made his father act like the benign child? He is still in this situation and asks, 'Why?'

Michel speaks of his regret in not understanding what his father was going through, but more positively says that this has helped him to shape what he wants to do with his life now. He is the editor of *Pendulum* – the journal of MDF The Bipolar Organization.

It has been an absolute pleasure and an inspiration to meet Michel. He finishes our meeting by saying, 'My most positive recent thought is to pull this off – my life, my forthcoming marriage and my future.'

Conclusion

I would like to take this opportunity to draw out some common factors experienced by every contributor's story. I must admit that I found this particular chapter incredibly difficult to write – I shed too many tears and I once too often had to skip to another chapter until I felt composed enough to continue with this one. I have revisited this chapter for one last time to conclude with the following points.

The children

- All the children admit that their mother's bipolar disorder has had an effect on their lives.

- Many mention that their school work was affected.

- All the children express an unconditional love towards their mothers.

- Many express some form of fear attached to their situation.

- Most of the children express that they have to take on a parental role at times.

- All the children appear to get upset when their mother is spending time crying and being in bed for long periods of time.

- Many of the children express their loneliness and confusion.

- Many of the children express their sadness and feelings of helplessness.

- Gina, David and James focus on the positive aspects of their mother's disorder and how they have had to mature quickly. They also explain how the situation with their mum has moulded them into who they are today.

- Gina, David, James and Bethan speak positively about their relationship with their mothers. They all say that they're proud and that they have the best mum in the world.

The adult children

- All the contributors in this section were keen to discuss their experience of growing up with a bipolar parent in order to help others.

- They all express that their parent's disorder has had a big impact on their adult lives.

- Sandy and Michel have developed bipolar disorder themselves.

- In Debbie's account, although she is heartbroken, she explains that she understands 'why' her father committed suicide.

- All the contributors speak about taking on the parental role.

- Most of them do fear inheriting bipolar and crave 'normality'.

- Most express the fact that they went through the illness alongside their parent.

- All say they remember their parent spending excessive time in bed.

- Michel and Sandy express their forgiveness towards their parent as they are experiencing the illness themselves.

- Many of the contributors lost trust in their parent and express how the inconsistency of their parent's moods was difficult.

- All of them clearly remember their parent's hospital admissions.

- Most of the contributors found very little, if any, information about bipolar disorder when they were young.

5
CHAPTER

Adult Relationships and Bipolar Disorder

In this chapter, I explore the challenges that can arise in relationships between adult members of a family. I discuss the common issues before providing a detailed account which represents a spectrum of perspectives written by different individuals within my own family, and the chapter goes on to feature a range of different experiences provided by contributors and their families.

When a family member has bipolar disorder, the illness can have a profound effect on the whole family. Bipolar disorder can raise a lot of negative emotions for the carer due to the erratic behaviour their loved one exhibits. It can often create feelings of anger, confusion, rejection and a general feeling of hopelessness and helplessness.

On occasions, it can prove impossible to plan anything ahead of time due to the varying episodes of the sufferer's mood. This can lead to you losing your social life, which in turn can make you feel extremely lonely and isolated.

Bipolar disorder is an extremely complex illness, and so it's important that everyone in the family learns as much about the illness as possible in order to know what you are dealing with. It is not easy to support a loved one when they are acting completely out of character, especially if you do not understand why. The more you understand about the illness, the better prepared you will be when an episode arises.

Supporting a person with bipolar disorder who is very ill can prove exhausting, often to the point where you can neglect your own needs. It is essential for all family members to look after themselves, because if you become ill, you will be unable to care for anyone else. Taking steps towards maintaining your own interests and hobbies is essential in order to stay fit and well.

Joining a self-help group is a good way to increase your support network in a friendly environment. Families will be able to help each other by sharing advice on coping mechanisms, swapping important information and even making new friends in a similar situation to them. Organizations such as MDF The Bipolar Organization in the UK or the Depression and Bipolar Support Alliance in the USA often have lists of local self-help groups.

It is helpful if family members are made aware of the medications and professional contacts of the person with bipolar disorder – being aware of these is a huge step towards helping to manage the disorder. It is highly recommended to approach these issues with great tact. The wishes of the person with bipolar disorder should be respected and they should make it clear to professionals if they want their family to be involved. It is important that the person, or 'patient' in this context, puts this in writing so it can be held on their file.

When a person with bipolar disorder is well, it can be a good idea for a family member to take the opportunity to sit down with them in a calm environment, to discuss the varying changes in mood. This will help to provide the family member with the knowledge of recognizing the early symptoms of each episode which can aid fast recovery.

I hope that you will find the different perspectives that follow as enlightening as I have done. I have learnt more than I thought possible by reading these contributions, and they have given me a far wider understanding by demonstrating just how many similarities exist between many families.

Adult relationships and bipolar disorder: Cara's family

It is probably helpful at this point to introduce my family to you in a little more detail. Basil is my partner. My mother is Marlene. Terry and Jody Austen are my father and stepmum. Lauren is my younger sister and Mark is my elder brother.

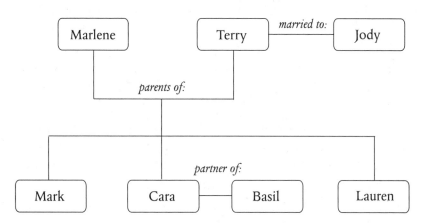

Adult relationships and bipolar disorder: Cara

I am scared of the dark. Very scared. Always have been, still am. I cannot sleep in a dark room. But once upon a time, about ten years ago, I found myself in the darkest of dark places.

Life became particularly difficult prior to my diagnosis. I was ill, very ill and very 'mad'. Having used the term 'mad' lightly in the past to describe someone as being 'funny', it became apparent to me that I was not funny, not funny at all. I completely lost sight of who I was. If I couldn't work out who I was, how on earth could I expect anyone else to? But I did. This expectation caused me to resent my husband, my whole family and many friends – they didn't understand, they looked confused, they tried to hold me up, they failed.

My sanity lay in tatters around me. I could not even recognize my own reflection staring back at me – a stranger, dark hollow eyes, sunken cheeks, a vision of madness. I had fallen from grace.

My family were beside themselves. They were totally confused by the situation. I listened to them all tell me, 'You really must try to pull yourself together, for the sake of the children.' This was not possible. I was admitted to hospital. I was discharged from hospital, I was readmitted. And on it goes.

After my first manic episode, I received my diagnosis of bipolar disorder. I had a little knowledge about the illness, but had a whole lot more to learn. My family relied on my knowledge. I had little to offer. I had to live with bipolar for a very long time before I could educate myself. My marriage broke down within the first year of my diagnosis. In turn, that damaged my relationship with my children, as they remained with their dad. I fell out with relatives, many friendships fell apart. In such a short space of time, my life had shattered into a million pieces. I felt as though I would never survive the storm. But as each day turned to night, and I prayed that this was just a bad dream, the sun rose upon another day. Somehow, and I don't know from where, I found an amazing strength within myself, to fight like I had never fought before...

Years later, having wasted all those 'yesterdays', and having survived all those dreaded 'tomorrows', I am incredibly proud of the fact that I now know who I am, where I am, where I have been, who I have lost, who I have gained and who I can trust. It takes most people a whole lifetime to work all this out. I did it in a decade.

Yes, I lost some friends. But the friends I do have are the best friends I could ever wish for. My relationship with my ex-husband is one of great friendship.

My family try their hardest to understand more about bipolar disorder. I find it very difficult and upsetting that when I have a manic episode some of them still say, 'Oh good, we have the old Cara back.' They do not recognize that the 'manic Cara' is an 'ill Cara', being driven by mania.

In general, the dimensions of my relationships within my family have changed somewhat. I'm much closer to my sister Lauren than ever before, she is wonderful. I've always been close to my mum, but I felt it was important to put a few boundaries in place. I had to do this in order to have a healthy 'mother/daughter' relationship, as opposed to a 'friendship'. I need a mum. I have a close relationship to my father and stepmother, and feel extremely supported by them. My in-laws have been fantastic.

My brother, Mark, who I was always extremely close to, I don't spend very much time with. I sometimes wonder if he doesn't truly understand my bipolar, or is frightened by it. It must be hard for him to see me suffering. I don't mind, I still love him very much. Being so close in age, we had so much fun throughout our childhood and teenage years. We went everywhere together, and shared the same circle of friends. We ran our family home, we were a good team. I did the 'girls' jobs'; he did the 'boys' jobs'. We were best buddies. I grieve for those wonderful years of growing up with my brother, and would like to turn the clock back, just for one single day, to recapture, and remember with clarity, a fabulous time in my life.

It's a sad fact, but bipolar disorder not only destroys the mind; unfortunately, due to a general lack of understanding, it can also destroy the dynamics of relationships.

I don't expect anyone to completely 'understand' me. At times, even I cannot make the grade!

My sister, Lauren, came under my wrath for quite some time. I misunderstood her for far too long. She was the one who took my children in, as her own, when I was so frequently ill. She would move heaven and earth to accommodate my girls. She even made my youngest daughter, Tasha, her very own bedroom at her home, as she spent so much time there. She bought her the most beautiful quilt cover. I had been feeling like a worthless human being and a dreadful mother during this long period of illness. Tasha idolized my sister. She became Tasha's role model for a mother. I became jealous – perhaps more hurt, that I could not offer my own daughter the same stability that my sister could.

Last year, my sister moved house. I had recovered from a very long and serious relapse and was back on my feet. Lauren gave me the quilt cover for Tasha's bed. Do you think I can put that cover on Tasha's bed without crying? No, I can't. I will never be able to do that 'dry eyed'. Why? Because my wonderful sister never once deserved the times I shouted at her, screamed at her, or the occasions I made her cry. She is without doubt, the very best. She deserves the world.

I would like to clarify that despite bipolar disorder 'steaming up my lenses' just that little too often, I can clearly make sense of what has been destructive, and of what has been constructive. I would like to set aside the destructive side, and focus on everything I have been lucky enough to have gained over the past ten years.

The most positive aspects of my illness are the people I have met while in a psychiatric hospital. I was always warned not to exchange phone numbers with another psychiatric patient. I did. Thank God I did.

I found a soul mate in my very great friend Sandy, who I met in hospital. She suffers from bipolar disorder too, and has contributed to this book. We are just approaching a milestone together. Ten years of friendship. A 'forever' friendship where our lives run parallel. Someone who 'lives' these episodes with me. Someone who can make me 'belly laugh' at *all* times. We share a crazy mind in this very crazy world.

Basil arrived in my life when neither he, nor I, knew just how much we needed each other. He was a young, very sensitive, quiet and shy person, who I found myself looking out for, on my twice weekly outpatient visits at the hospital. Somehow, we fell comfortably into a routine of sitting and chatting the afternoons away during those beautiful summer months. We were just two people, being one, holding each other up through thick and thin. I 'loved' Basil from the first time I met him – not in an 'in love' sense, but I just knew he was an exceptionally special person. He has proven that to me over and over again since. We have a beautiful, easy friendship – one I don't think I'll ever experience with anybody else in my life. It took a long time, and a lot of trust on both sides, but we did fall in love, although I don't think either of us realized it at first. I can only describe Basil as the most beautiful human being put on this earth, inside and out. He has continually held me up, stopped me from falling apart, and at times has kept me alive. He has loved me to pieces, loved my children as his own, and makes me so very happy, each and every day. Basil is my rock.

There really are no words powerful enough to describe the love I feel for my daughters. Despite my illness, I have an extremely close relationship with both Georgina (who is 19) and Tasha (who is 15). They understand me, accept me totally for 'me', and love me unconditionally, as I do them. We have so much fun together, they make me laugh, I make them laugh, and our home is always a very happy one. I feel so blessed to have such beautifully natured girls. I can say, with great pride, that they both have beautiful souls.

The girls, together with Basil, give me the strength to bounce back, each and every time I fall.

I am very lucky.

Adult relationships and bipolar disorder: Basil

Cara and I met when we were both patients at a psychiatric hospital. I was suffering from depression and anxiety, and she had recently been diagnosed with bipolar disorder. During the first few years of our relationship, Cara suffered from depression and anxiety, and if she experienced an episode of mania, it wouldn't last for more than a few days. I found I was able to care for her well, as I had experienced many of the symptoms myself. Her illness was made all the worse as she had become addicted to Valium (diazepam), for which she was later treated. I soon realized that once Cara had taken her night-time medication, I was responsible for both her and her daughters. There were times when her daughters, Gina and Tasha, would wake up during the night not feeling well and try to wake Cara up. Cara would still be affected by her medication and she would not know what she was saying. She would sometimes tell them to take the wrong medication when they were ill, so I had to be there for them.

There were times early on in the relationship when Cara was ill, when she was unable to look after Gina and Tasha. The girls would often go to stay with their dad, Roo. Tasha seemed to be understanding and would go willingly, but Gina would often react with anger and would shout at Cara. Without the responsibility of her daughters, Cara was able to medicate and then sleep off the effects of the medication. After a few days rest, Cara was then able to look after the girls again. I was aware that this was very difficult for the girls to have to cope with. If the girls had friends over, the friends would have to be made aware that Cara was ill as she would cry and need to sleep off medication.

At one stage, the psychiatrist looking after her wanted to change Cara's medication as it was an old type of medication and there were newer more effective medications available. I said to the psychiatrist that it was not necessary to alter Cara's medication at this period of time, as Cara was well. The psychiatrist insisted that Cara went into hospital to change the medication. The medication change appeared to go smoothly and Cara was home after ten days.

Unfortunately, soon after coming home, Cara began to suffer long periods of mania which developed into a mixed state episode. At this point, the psychiatrist was no longer able to care for Cara as he believed that she required treatment in hospital. Her doctor (GP), who has been fantastic in caring for Cara, referred her to the local mental health unit. An appointment was made for a few weeks later, but I could see her mood deteriorating. I became more concerned for Cara and called the mental health unit to have the appointment brought forward. It took forever, but eventually the GP had the appointment brought forward.

A new psychiatrist at the mental health unit tried to reintroduce Cara's original medication. This had no effect and Cara's mental health became worse. During this period, Cara and I tried to protect her daughters from the illness, as much as was possible.

In the meantime, Cara had carried out research and found that there was a Professor Farmer at the Maudsley Hospital who specialized in bipolar disorder. Cara asked her current psychiatrist for a referral, however, the local NHS trust was reluctant to fund it due to budget restraints. After a couple of months, the psychiatrist eventually got the referral to see Professor Farmer. During the assessment, she outlined a plan of action and advised for Cara to start new medications. I could see that Cara's recovery would take many months.

During this period, I could see that both her daughters were badly affected by Cara's ongoing illness. Tasha and Gina would not want to sit with Cara and myself and would spend most of their time in their bedroom on their computers. Tasha took a lot of time off from school, as she was too upset to go. I can relate to Tasha not wanting to be at school, as when I was at work, I would be unable to concentrate on work, as I was worried about Cara. Gina suffered from anxiety and experienced chest pains and irritable bowel syndrome. Both girls would often argue with each other, which was an understandable reaction to the bipolar disorder.

After the meeting with Professor Farmer, I felt I had to be honest with Gina and Tasha. So when I had the chance to talk to them alone, I said to them that I believed that it would take months for their mother to get better, and for things to get back to normal. Gina took this badly as she thought Cara would be better within a matter of weeks. I also said to the girls that I believed they were both badly affected by Cara's illness and that they should consider spending more time with their dad. I said this because I love the girls so much, and did not want to see them suffer. Both Gina and Tasha said they were unaffected by their mum's illness and would not want to be anywhere else.

During this relapse, I never stopped loving Cara. It pained me to see her suffering. We stopped going out socially, and Cara had stopped saying she loved me. Normally Cara and I are very loving towards each other but we stopped kissing and cuddling. I began to feel very lonely. The only person I felt able to confide in was my mother. Although I love Cara's family, I felt unable to talk to them as they were so worried about her and seemed to be more affected by her illness than myself, even though they did not witness the worst aspects of the bipolar disorder.

There have been two times during our relationship when I have not been able to cope with Cara's bipolar. These have both been when Cara has become suicidal. On the first occasion, Cara was under the care of the crisis team, who were very supportive.[6] If I had not insisted that Cara come to bed that night, she told me she would have taken a load of her pills in order to end her life. The second occasion was when Cara was experiencing suicidal thoughts for a very long period and the children didn't want to be away from her. Both Cara and I needed to have some respite, but this was not possible. I was experiencing chest pains from the anxiety, not sleeping well and I was beginning to feel depressed myself. Cara had no sympathy for how I was feeling and would say things like, 'Now you know how I feel.' I felt unloved, I felt that Cara no longer cared for me and I felt unsupported by her family. Cara and I had an argument and I went to stay with my mother. It was never my intention to end our relationship, but I could no longer cope with Cara's illness. After a few days I came back. I left, not because I stopped loving Cara, Gina or Tasha, but because I could not cope with Cara's suicidal thoughts on my own.

Slowly, Cara's mood lifted and she is fairly stable on her new medication. Both Gina and Tasha appear to be happier within themselves. I am now in contact with a mental health carers support group. I feel, should the need arise, I can call them. I also feel that now the girls are that much older, I am able to talk to them more openly and honestly.

I adore Cara, Gina and Tasha. They are my world.

Adult relationships and bipolar disorder: Lauren

This is about the third attempt I have had at writing this. Cara asked me to put into my own words how her illness affects me; it's much harder to do than anticipated. Firstly I don't want to upset anyone and secondly my coping mechanism

6   A crisis team is an educated team of people in psychiatric care who visit the individual in their own home up to twice a day. They support the patient at home to prevent a hospital admission where possible. They talk, listen, have access to doctors, psychiatrists and community psychiatric nurses at all times. They have 24-hour helplines for the patient they are assigned to.

doesn't allow me to bring my bad thoughts and memories to the forefront of my mind, but only to store it all up in a dark place somewhere behind my brain where no one can see it.

I am angry that my sister and I were brought up by the same parents and yet I have the ability to lead a 'normal' life and Cara's life is so affected by mental illness. There are no explanations as to why our lives are so different and I think that is why I find it so hard to understand Cara's illness. Many times Cara has given me literature to read to help me to understand it, but I almost get scared to read it. Why? Because in truth, I don't want to understand it. I'm not sure why this is, but I do know that I do everything possible to make my children's lives as 'normal' as possible, and I just want to know that they are happy and free from mental illness, and that we can all enjoy ourselves and survive what life throws at us. Perhaps I just don't want the reality of mental illness hitting me in the face, and if I don't know too much about it, in my world, in a way, it doesn't even exist.

I wake up every day thinking of my sister and can't wait to speak to her on the telephone. However busy my day is, I will still try to speak to her, come what may. When we don't speak for a day or so, I miss her so much. At the same time, I am scared to ring her in case she is feeling bad that day. My shoulders tense as I dial her number and it's such a relief when I know she is OK, and such a horrible feeling when she's not.

Sometimes I get impatient with her when she is not well and I get off the telephone feeling awful pangs of guilt. Then the next day I will ring her again with a different mindset but more often than not, I will still be impatient with her if she's still not well. I don't want to be like that, but I find it all so draining. I am selfish; but I really don't want to be only I can't seem to help it. I want my sister to be 'normal' and for her girls not to know what mental illness is.

The girls: my biggest worry. Over the years I have done as much as possible to support them. I love knowing that the girls are happy to be around me and feel safe with me.

In my opinion, they shouldn't be experiencing Cara's mood swings and sometimes her tears for days on end. They need the stability of our family, the family behind my front door. As the girls have got older I have observed that the older one is suffering from bouts of depression which breaks my heart. I worry about her but can't seem to talk about it.

Selfishly again I know I can look after the girls, supporting Cara at the same time, without really having to spend time with her. That sounds awful, but I always feel the need to distance myself when Cara is ill. I never know what to say to her and I can't listen to the same symptoms over and over again. I find it difficult to discuss her medication and her doctors' names and what they have said to her this time. This, I believe, stems back to our mum, a mum who is always complaining of one illness after another, constantly naming medication, doctors, symptoms, etc. For me, I back off as soon as the conversation starts. I actually find it quite stressful and almost shut my ears.

Perhaps I am ignorant, selfish, a martyr, all the things I have been labelled over the years. But I would rather be those things than suffer like my sister does. I take on so much in life and I am sure the reason for this is to prove something to myself. To prove I can cope, that I am strong. Sometimes I can't cope and I'm not strong either. I just have the ability to cover it up for my children's sakes.

I love my sister with all my heart and I know she feels the same about me. I wish I could do something that would cure her of mental illness, but I can't. All I can do is be there for her and try to ease the burden. She is the most wonderful person and I am very lucky to have her in my life. My biggest fear is that one day she may just be pushed over the edge and take her life. I couldn't go on if she did that. Apart from my children, she is the most special, important person to me and I wouldn't be able to cope with that; there would certainly be no covering up my feelings then. I don't even think I would be capable of looking after the girls. It doesn't bear thinking about so I will just do the usual, and put that thought into the dark place where it belongs.

Mental illness is apparently a chemical imbalance; true, I am sure, but I also believe it's genetic and/or is triggered by a traumatic event.

Adult relationships and bipolar disorder: Marlene

My daughter was always like a ray of sunshine – smiling and happy all the time. She was a very positive person who 'adopted' all the waifs and strays, and brought happiness to their lives. She worked in my recruitment business and had an excellent rapport with all of my temporary staff (which I supplied to companies in and around the City of London). Everyone was drawn to her and her radiant personality.

She was married and had been trying to have a baby for a few years, which did not happen. However, she became very ill and the doctors found that her bowel was twisted. They operated on her very successfully, but in a matter of about a month or so, she started to haemorrhage, and was rushed to Accident and Emergency (Emergency Room) at a hospital near her. It was after a full examination that they found she was pregnant, but had miscarried. I expected her to be devastated, but instead, she looked up at me smiling and said, 'At least I know I can conceive now.' That was how positive she was.

It was once she actually did have children that she developed severe postnatal depression which, in those days, was not as talked about as now. She tried to hide it all the time, but it did take its toll on her. Eventually she was able to enjoy her children, and gave them extra love and time, in order to make up for the time she was 'unwell'.

I tried to be there for her, but as I had my business to run, I couldn't be with her as much as I wanted to. I felt absolutely useless as I felt I had let her down.

Cara lived in a bungalow which backed onto playing fields, and had a gate from her garden to the fields. It was when she was walking her beloved dog Yanni, that she saw two large Alsatians attack her, and she couldn't do anything but scream. Yanni died during that night. It was after that experience that her moods started to change drastically.

She seemed to be very low for days or weeks on end, and then, suddenly, she would be 'high in the sky'. She was admitted to hospital on several occasions before she was diagnosed as having bipolar disorder. Even then, it took years to get any form of medication to stabilize her. We were all devastated, but me, as her mother, more so. All I knew was that I wanted my darling sunny child back again, and that I couldn't do anything to help her. The feeling of uselessness on my part continued and did take a toll on me.

It was during this awful period that she and her husband separated. He is a lovely man, but he could not handle the way she was. It was then that my daughter stayed with me, until she could find a flat to move into.

Her children were staying with their father, Roo, most of the week, and with Cara a couple of nights. The girls were desperately unhappy, and so was my daughter that she could not 'cope' with them for long periods of time. My granddaughters were nine and four respectively and, of course, they wanted to be with their mother.

It was an awful period in Cara's life, the children's lives, and of course, my life. I am certain it was also very painful for Roo, Cara's husband. Everyone loved her, but we all felt so very helpless. It affected my concentration and therefore my work. All I could think of was my daughter and adorable grandchildren.

Cara had always loved to light candles around her home, making it look cheery and welcoming. However, my elder grandchild, Gina, couldn't sleep until Cara had gone to bed, as she wanted to make sure that all the candles were blown out before she could go to sleep. She began to carry out many 'safety rituals', both at her mummy's and daddy's houses.

When the children were with their daddy one night, he drank far too much and passed out. Gina phoned her mummy, panicking, and she went to fetch the children and take them home with her. It came out, at this point, that Gina had been helping her father to bed each night, to make certain he was safe. It got to such a stage that she slept in his bed, and had to put her arm over him to ensure he didn't fall out.

Gina suffered greatly during that period of time, so Cara was determined to take the girls back, and keep them with her more permanently, while their daddy straightened his drinking problem out. It didn't take him long at all, as he was so disgusted with himself for the problems he was causing, and took immediate steps to rectify his drinking habit. He is a lovely man, and now the girls stay with their mother most of the time and with their father once or twice a week.

I am their grandmother, and it was awful to be looking at this situation, and not being able to help any of them very much. I felt shell-shocked, and I could not sleep well, as I was afraid that I was going to get a bad phone call during the night.

My daughter has been in and out of hospital so many times, but now, thankfully, her mood swings are much less frequent than they were, and she manages (with lots of medication) to keep most of them under control. However, many times she has to take very strong medication to enable her to sleep and therefore 'get through' the rough times.

She has a wonderful partner whom she met whilst in one of the hospitals, where he was an outpatient. They have lived together for a number of years now, and because he has been through depression himself, he can understand, and help her through the tough times. Also, he is wonderful with the girls, and treats them as if they were his own.

It is awful standing by and watching your child go from a happy-go-lucky child and teenager, into someone who seems so troubled, and who has such irrational thoughts.

She worries when the children are out, and as Gina drives now, Cara does not go to sleep until she knows Gina is back home safely. If either of the children is staying out, she will not sleep until she receives a text or call telling her they are back safely.

Both children's friends enjoy being at Cara's house, and she absolutely loves the company of youngsters around her. She is so young at heart, and between Cara and Basil, they always cook tons of food, never knowing how many are going to be there for dinner. She gets great enjoyment out of seeing all of the kids sitting around and laughing and joking. All of the girls' friends say they wish they had a mother like her – welcoming everyone who comes round and making them feel as though her home is their home.

Cara is a remarkable person, giving so much love to everyone. She and her ex-husband are great friends, and Cara's partner, Basil, understands their friendship completely. Basil has a very warm and inviting nature, which is welcoming to anyone who comes to their home. I still worry about Cara so much, but I feel better knowing she has such a great partner who is there for her whenever and whatever.

It is still very hard when I see her suffering, when she is down, or indeed, when she is too high, but it is now far less frequent, and we all seem to recognize symptoms before an episode happens.

The children, also, are now of an age where they understand their mother's bipolar and are more able to cope.

Adult relationships and bipolar disorder: Terry and Jody

The following account is written by Cara's father, Terry, and stepmother, Jody.

The hidden fear of this mental illness, and the effect it has on all our family, is hard to understand. It is difficult to comprehend how our loving, caring and lively daughter could change so dramatically with massive mood swings and depressions. For us, not being able to do anything to ease the situation that is ongoing for long periods is difficult.

When Cara was first taken into a psychiatric clinic, I could not understand what was happening and found this very hard to accept. Jody was very patient and a lot more understanding of the situation. She helped me to, very slowly, come round and find some sort of reason for this trauma, as things were improving and even though Cara was still having mood swings of highs and lows.

We tried to analyse why this had happened to Cara, as did her psychiatrist and nurses. The condition seemed to be deep-rooted, but took a long time to diagnose. With medication and treatment, Cara began to get control over her illness, but will never be cured. We have had to understand and accept her as she is and, despite her bipolar, she is still a loving and caring daughter and an excellent mother to her children.

When she is well, we can only hope she will get better and better. Only time and patience will tell.

We will always be there for her because of the love we have for her.

Despite everything, the most important thing to have come out of this illness is Cara meeting Basil in the psychiatric clinic. He has been a fantastic support throughout, not only to her, but also to the children.

Adult relationships and bipolar disorder: Sandy Knox

Sandy is mother to Tom and partner of Tel.

My bipolar doesn't seem to bother my boyfriend. He says he's learned to live with it. He says he doesn't notice it any more, like he doesn't notice when I'm not wearing make-up. It's part of me, he says, it's who I am. He finds me amusing and interesting like a curio. I am his muse, he says. But when I'm really down and scared it hurts him. He says he feels my pain, and is clueless as to how to help me. Sometimes he just has to go home and I have to ride it out on my own. Sometimes he holds me and tells me everything will be all right. But that's what living with it is all about, everyone's affected. On the whole though, he is not bothered, doesn't notice, and can't see what's right in front of his nose. But that's just a man thing, isn't it, thank God, I must be a nightmare!

Adult relationships and bipolar disorder: Tracey's family

Adult relationships and bipolar disorder: Tracey

Tracey is mother to David, James and Bethan, and wife of Rob.

I have been married to Rob for 23 years. He finds it hard when he can't predict my moods. When I've been 'doped up' with medication, he knows what to expect, but now my moods swing more frequently. Rob is brilliant and will do anything for me, but has a somewhat controlling streak. In the summer, he left home for two weeks due to the pressures of work. I cried endlessly for two days, but then found a strength I never knew I had. I realized that Rob had squashed me, rather than him controlling my highs. He now calls me 'his butterfly' as he realized, while he was away, that I had been withering, and he needs to leave my 'cage' open. He was awarded Carer of the Year by The Wave and Swansea Sound radio stations, beating 400 entries in Wales.

I do have an elder brother, but he never shows affection, although he has offered to look after Bethan for a week in the past. The other members of my family offer no support at all, except for my mother-in-law, who has been very supportive.

Adult relationships and bipolar disorder: Rob

I met Tracey at a Bible study group at St Helen's Church, Bishopsgate, London whilst I was at university. She was very pretty, with dark-brown, shoulder-length hair and sparkly, mischievous, brown eyes. I must confess that I was very pleased to see her join our group!

Over the next couple of years, we got to know each other as good friends, but without a hint of romance. Our Bible study leader encouraged us to keep in touch with each other whilst I was on placement in the Midlands and we wrote to each other, but there was still no romance. Then, on my return to London, we met up at church and I saw her home after the evening service. Tracey invited me in for a coffee and a piece of toast. She later told me that she looked into my blue eyes that night over the toaster and was smitten! I am a bit odd-looking and at the time had a particularly poor hairstyle. However, my eyes are two of my better features and that night they were responsible for a dramatic change in both of our lives.

Tracey had been quite hurt by the break-up with a previous boyfriend and had asked God to keep men away until Mr Right came along. Consequently that revelation over the toaster came as a bit of a shock. Over the following weeks, Tracey dropped various hints, but I was completely oblivious to them. Finally, in desperation, during a walk she uttered the immortal words: 'I fancy you' and 'I would like to go out with you!' 'Oh,' I said, 'Can I think about it?'

Never the great romantic and comfortable with our friendship, the question came as a bit of a shock to me. Furthermore, as one who tends to procrastinate, I didn't ask her out until several weeks later and even when I did, did not make my intentions clear. It was only the day after our first date, when I confirmed to one of her friends that we were going out, that she responded by saying, 'It is nice of you to let me know!' We started the way we meant to continue and have been communicating perfectly ever since!

A few weeks after we started going out together, I was diagnosed with cancer. God was so loving to me at that time: he gave me amazing peace as I knew that if I died I was going to a much better place and if I survived I would be able to enjoy life all the more. He also put wonderful Christians in my path at that time, such as Tracey. In many ways the illness brought us closer together.

Then, soon after my recovery, Tracey's mum was diagnosed with cancer and tragically died within weeks. She was only 45. Her mother's death had a very profound effect on Tracey and, even now, there are still times when waves of grief overwhelm her.

She fell behind with her studies and finished her nursing training early. She went home to help her dad with the family business, but after a few weeks had to be admitted to a psychiatric unit, suffering from depression.

By this time, Tracey and I were engaged and I remember discussing with my father what I should do.

'I love her, Dad.'

'Well, in that case,' replied my father, 'marry her!'

It was good advice and once Tracey was better, we got married.

That was almost 25 years ago and during that time we have experienced some amazing highs and desperate lows. The Bible states that when a couple marry, the two become one flesh. So when Tracey has been struck by the extremes of bipolar, it has had a profound effect on me as well. Quite often it has pushed me in the opposite direction in order to try to regain some level of control. This rarely works and generally makes things worse. At times, I have felt stretched to the limit, but God has been gracious and in many respects I am a better person for going through these trials.

Tracey is incredibly talented, with a wonderful zany sense of humour and, despite her health problems, she has been a very loving and supportive wife, a great mum and a good friend to many people. I love her to bits and thank God for her.

Adult relationships and bipolar disorder: Karen Paige

Karen is the mother of two children, aged 14 and 10. She discusses her experience of parenting with bipolar disorder in Chapter 3.

I don't know how my ex-partner would look at it, but I think my illness had a part to play in the breakdown of my relationship with the father of my son. My ex had not really experienced any adversity in his life. We got together after four years of friendship when my daughter was two. Simultaneously with the decision to move in together I found out that I was pregnant. A week after my son's birth, I became barking mad (with undiagnosed bipolar disorder), and was convinced that my son was the Messiah. My partner stood by me, and even proposed while I was an inpatient. Maybe a little misguided, but I think the sentiment was to show that he would always be there. Recovery in its truest term was arduous. There were other trials in our relationship, and I think that, in the end, my partner bagged it all together, and thought that it was too much hard work being with me. Life hadn't thrown these things at him before he was with me, and with that, he decided that leaving me might be a good idea.

It isn't that straightforward though and I guess the relationship didn't stand the test of trials because fundamentally things weren't right. The way I understand it is that when, under the doctors' instruction, I discontinued my lithium, it was like I took dark glasses off and some invisible weight had been lifted. I started asking questions about my experience of my illness. Basically I found that my partner had, in my eyes, betrayed my trust.

The issue was electroconvulsive therapy (ECT). The doctors were sure that this treatment would result in a quick recovery. I feared it would destroy my memory and change my personality. My concern was based on the ill effects ECT had had on my grandmother. I had only agreed to this course of treatment as my partner had told me he had researched it independently. I discovered this to be untrue. I felt as if I had been raped. I stopped trusting and desolation set in to the relationship, culminating in his leaving.

Bipolar has affected my subsequent relationships because of my low self-esteem. I find myself with men that reinforce that. I felt so much like tarnished goods after the second manic episode that I settled for another relationship where I wasn't made to feel special. I tried to make up for the relationship with my son's dad by not being demanding. Really, looking back, I was a bit of a doormat. It's hard to recognize where the fire I had previously had gone in this relationship. I suppose I just felt that I would have to settle with this rather boring man, and a relationship in which I felt plain and boring. This relationship ended. The situation now is that I have been very independent, not feeling I can rely on those around. I feel very different because of the experience of the propensity for madness; I find it hard to trust. I feel detached and different, making it hard to get close to anyone. I can chat but inside it's hard to keep my guard down.

In the normal course of events, I see my mother regularly. I don't really talk about my feelings or problems, but she is generally around and helpful with the children. My dad lives further away and our relationship is a bit detached. The interesting thing is that when things are in crisis, it's my dad who I turn to, not my mum. My mum just gets flustered and is unable to think through things when I can't think myself. She's unable to help me take steps to calm the situation.

My dad has a physical illness which means he has to take it easy, but he is able to talk me through my meandering thoughts. He encourages me so that I do not have to act on every single thought which would result in me going round and round in circles. My dad is the relative I feel closest to and we have talked about what this means. I do have faith that he would make decisions based on his own judgement of what is right for me, rather than being swayed by mental health professionals.

Adult relationships and bipolar disorder: Jo Bell's family

Adult relationships and bipolar disorder: Jo Bell

Jo is mother to Malachi, and fiancé of David.

I feel very fortunate to have such a strong relationship with my partner, David, and that he fully understands and accepts the fact that my bipolar is a part of my life.

On the subject of my parents, unfortunately my father died, and my mother and I had difficulties. She found it very difficult in the earlier stages of my diagnosis, to the point where I thought she had no interest in me since I developed bipolar disorder. My grandparents and my uncle get scared when I have a manic episode, so I spend time with them all when I am well.

Many of my friends were scared off during my manic episodes; others simply believe I had a nervous breakdown. But even after you take them all out of the equation, I'm lucky enough to still have a small group of close friends who now laugh with me about all that has happened. They've all read the leaflets and researched bipolar disorder on the internet.

Adult relationships and bipolar disorder: Sue

Sue is Jo Bell's mother.

What's going on? I don't understand, what do I do? I didn't know enough about the situation I was in and needed to get my daughter expert help. This resulted in her being sectioned and it was considered my fault. My daughter released all her venom on me and I was the devil incarnate. I was the face she focused on and she hit me with both barrels. I knew I had done right but God, it was hard. This was my flesh and blood.

Jo started to accept treatment and was diagnosed as having bipolar disorder. What a relief! This was treatable and there was hope that I would get my daughter back. She has continued to receive treatment and we now laugh about what happened at the time of this episode. I have promised to slap her next time it happens! It was a scary, frightening, unsettling time but we have come through it. I am so proud of her and the way she now copes with it. We both now understand what happened, and may happen in the future. I have never known her so happy and hope this continues. There are no guarantees but at least, next time, we know what we are dealing with. Unfortunately it's like living with a volcano, you hope it doesn't happen but you know it could erupt at any time.

Adult relationships and bipolar disoder: David

Life with a bipolar partner is very unpredictable. I often find myself wondering what I have done wrong only to find later that nothing is the matter. Jo requires a lot more of my attention than I ever anticipated when I first met her. We discussed not so long ago what I would say if she were offered a one-shot cure. I wouldn't have her any other way. The ups and downs of life are greatly exaggerated with Jo. This to me though is a good thing. Too often in life, people and the lives they lead are humdrum, boring and average. With Jo everything is an adventure. Thick skin and patience are handy attributes to have with a bipolar partner. Only now, after a couple of years, Jo is starting to explore her existence without constantly limiting her field of view to bipolar disorder.

The condition and the extra planning it requires can be quite all-consuming and it would be easy for one to get lost in the whirlwind. All I can advise any person about to go through the grief Jo has suffered, is to hang on for the ride because it makes people extraordinary. There are aspects of Jo that she doesn't see as the sufferer, an inner strength that comes from the daily fight with her own mind. My suggestion to her and to all would be simple: have faith and love each other. Everything else is secondary!

Adult relationships and bipolar disorder: Phaedra Excell

Phaedra is mother to Amy and is married to Mark.

Having bipolar disorder has affected my relationship with my family, in that I feel like I cannot totally trust them. My younger sister in particular seems to enjoy trying to hurt my feelings. She has done it so many times that it's just become irritating and tedious. It seems as though she tries to make me become manic – maybe to make herself look better. She's always telling me to stop taking all my medicine, and that taking everything is poisoning me and that I don't need it. My sister always tries to sabotage my happiness and stability. She's the middle child who views my life as perfect, due to the fact that my husband makes plenty of money, I don't have to work and I've got a university degree. These are things she doesn't possess. But, like many people, I have plenty to be upset about, and my life is very far from perfect.

When I was diagnosed, my husband Mark did lots of research about bipolar disorder instead of simply thinking 'it was all in my head'. Mark is my main support beam; he monitors my moods, since it's very difficult to be introspective when my moods start to get severe or change. He's never told me to get a job, or that I'm lazy because the house is a mess. He is absolutely wonderful and I can't imagine getting through this without him helping me.

Fortunately, I have been honest about my bipolar with my friends, so they know that when they don't hear from me for a long time, it's because I'm going through a hard time and that I'll be in touch with them when I feel better.

I have included the following two accounts to demonstrate some of the difficulties involved with caring for a bipolar spouse.

Adult relationships and bipolar disorder: Paul and Claire Edwards

The following account is by Paul's wife, Claire. Paul discusses his experience of life with bipolar disorder in Chapter 2.

My name is Claire Edwards and I am a carer for my husband Paul, who suffers with bipolar disorder. I think you have to have stamina and guts, and be strong, not only for the person affected, but for yourself as well. If you crack, then they could crack under the pressure too. When Paul is in one of his hypomanic stages, I do find it mentally and physically tiring, but you have to learn how to push the boundaries, and how to deal with certain situations. When Paul is down, I will just gently be in the background, monitoring his habits, but I won't try to cover him with love, so to speak. There is nothing worse than being smothered, but it's nice to know someone is always watching from a distance.

I believe there is not enough recognition for bipolar sufferers and their carers. Recently, a spate of newspaper articles have been reporting about celebrities who have been diagnosed with it. I feel that just because they want to get themselves out of their big holes, and their drink-fuelled appetites, they see bipolar as the latest fashion accessory, and choose to use it when it suits them. Whereas real bipolar sufferers and their carers physically need the help they can't get.

It is upsetting to see a once lovely husband who still is lovely, go from being hubbly and bubbly, to smack down more or less overnight. With bipolar can come a self-harm side and this is where I have to watch Paul. He has self-harmed to date around 12, 13, maybe 15 times, and on two of those occasions he tried to cut his wrists.

Basically, to cut a long story short, you need to let them know you are there for them in good times and bad. It's like marriage vows say: for better, for worse – well, there is one vow we are both living up to now.

I won't be the first and I certainly won't be the last to put my hand up and say I can't cope sometimes, because if anybody does, they are lying. You have to have coping strategies in place, and I like to play games when I get the time on the computer, whilst Paul is resting, or read a magazine, or take Paul out of the situation for a walk. But I am always nearby watching. To be honest, I believe that patients with bipolar are given a raw deal, but we must be the lucky ones. It has taken a file of paperwork between the Department of Work and Pensions and our local Member of Parliament to fight for Paul's case. Also, our doctor has been ever so supportive, and then finally we got the result we needed – an appointment with a senior psychiatrist and a bloody good CPN, who visits once a fortnight. We also have access to 24-hour support down the telephone line.

We are currently awaiting correspondence through a housing association, which will place Paul and me into a type of supported housing, where we can get more help with the day-to-day running of things, before Paul's illness worsens. I know many people who would run a mile, but I always believe that Paul and I will be together for a while yet.

Adult relationships and bipolar disorder: Andrew and Heather Heald

Heather speaks about 'Making a bipolar marriage work', drawing on her own experience of having a husband with bipolar disorder. This piece appeared in the Autumn 2007 edition of Pendulum *magazine (the journal of MDF The Bipolar Organization).*

A husband and wife relationship has different strengths and difficulties to one between a father and son or a mother and daughter. My husband told me, at the start of our relationship, that he had manic depression. The way I saw it was: he has the condition and he has it for life. I want to be with him. I must learn to deal with it. This element of choice is something that people in other types of relationships might not have.

Practical elements also need addressing, such as finances. We do not have rent or a mortgage or children (fortunately so, in our opinion). Nevertheless we have to watch our expenditure and have a modest lifestyle, never having holidays abroad and almost never having evenings out.

There are some tension points. One is my husband's severe tiredness. Sometimes he falls asleep by 7pm, frustrating when I have been in work all day. I deal with this by playing patience or playing chess on the computer. I'll make championship level one day – I don't think! Another irritation is that it is always me who has to deal with unwanted callers. I don't mind really as it gives me a valid reason to be bolshie. My husband refuses to take up arms in almost any situation – this is perhaps to the good because it balances my policy of 'shoot first and ask questions afterwards'.

In the aftermath of an episode of any type, he only wants to relax. We do this by enjoying togetherness, listening to classical music, going for walks, etc.

There is one thing in our situation that those in other situations will not have. If I need a listening ear, some might think, 'You knew he had it – don't complain.' No one has actually said this to me but some might think it. If so, let them. I have enough supportive people in my life not to care what the unsupportive think.

In conclusion, I can see that my husband's condition changed my horizons. Previously I was considering doing a PhD and hoping to get a job in academia. I could not cope with a pressurized job now.

But, I love my husband. We manage on our joint income. I like my part-time job with a very supportive group of colleagues. I wouldn't change a thing.

My philosophy is: if life gives you lemons, make lemonade.

Conclusion

In reading the material in this chapter, I have observed some common themes, both from the contributors and the families alike. I have noted some similarities below.

- The families of most of the contributors have feelings of confusion in the earlier stages of the diagnosis.

- It was very sad to read how most of the family spoke in the 'past tense', for example, 'My daughter used to be…'

- Many of the parents now express their admiration for their child and describe them as excellent parents.

- Marriage and relationship breakdowns are a common theme.

- Some of our friendships were broken, but a stronger bond developed with the friends who remained.

- Many of the contributors' partners, most of whom have been deeply affected by their loved one's disorder, still speak adoringly about them.

- In most of the accounts, the family members, and in particular the partners, have demonstrated their own strengths in dealing with their loved one's disorder. Many have said that they admire and are proud of their loved one's 'fight'.

6

CHAPTER

Bipolar Disorder and Society

I have left this chapter until the end of the book to show that, while the main focus of this book is on family life with a disorder, as families we are also affected by attitudes within the communities within which we life. This chapter provides an opportunity for the contributors to express their own experiences of how living with mental illness relates to living in today's society.

In reading through these accounts, you will see that a number of contributors recount disturbing experiences as patients in psychiatric hospitals. The individual experiences included here should be treated as such, and it's my intention that these passages act as a constructive way of highlighting where services or training are wanting. There are a lot of dedicated, caring and understanding mental health professionals, including those who write within this book, who have been a great source of support and advice.

Bipolar disorder and society: Cara

I must admit that, despite writing two books based on the subject of mental illness, I still feel totally judged by people on the fact that I have bipolar disorder. It's even worse when I have to label my disorder as 'manic depression' to those who don't understand the term 'bipolar disorder'. This, in turn, immediately has an effect on their opinion of me with a very visible change in their behaviour. Some almost back off before I have a chance to explain I'm not some lunatic, but an intelligent and often talented person despite my diagnosis.

Over the past 18 months I have suffered with ongoing problems related to a stomach operation which took place some 20 years ago. I have been hospitalized on numerous occasions and have spent many hours, at various times, in the Accident and Emergency Unit (Emergency Room) of our local hospital. The first question I am asked by the doctors involved is whether I am on any medication. Due to my bipolar, I have a rather long list of stabilizing medications. The doctors tend not to look further than the fact that I have bipolar, and I am often sent away as in their opinion my physical health appears to be related to my disorder rather than the stomach operation. They have no respect for me as an individual – they view my mental illness as a cause of a physical problem. It is obvious to me that the public and doctors alike lose respect for me as a person in my own right once my mental condition is known. This causes me great sadness and frustration about the fact that I am not 'Cara', but a person who suffers from mental illness.

On the occasions that I have had an admission to a psychiatric hospital, the staff have treated me in an appalling manner. I have been screamed at by the nurses to get up and dressed, despite the fact that my medication can knock me out for hours during the morning. It is frightening to have a nurse standing over me shouting and threatening me that I will not get a meal if I don't 'pull myself together'. I strongly question how the mental health service view an inpatient admission as the way forward to recovery. Each and every time I have ended up in hospital, I become aggressive, angry and far more ill than when I first arrived. I have had to beg for my discharge time and again. I have been at the receiving end of violent patients threatening me to the point to which it verges on abuse. I am not an aggressive person, I am not an angry person, I am placid, laid back, polite and very friendly. I hate the person I become when hospitalized.

I am, by nature, a very optimistic person and have to share one very funny story which occurred while I was in hospital last year. There was the most wonderful elderly male patient whom everyone disliked. I actually thought he was a very sweet man, despite the fact that he would regularly appear naked in the smoking room whenever I was in there.

He took great pride in showing me his colostomy bag and fiddling with it. He would then ask me to hold his hand. Not a nice prospect but I always held his hand (bless him)! One of my 'abusers' took a further dislike to me due to the fact that I befriended this old man whom he had taunted constantly. To add insult to injury, I then became stuck in the middle of a war between the two of them.

The most outstanding memory of my time in that very same hospital was when one of the violent patients decided to smash the whole ward to pieces. There were only two female nurses on duty on that particular night, who couldn't restrain this patient. Therefore, they locked themselves in the nurses station and left all the patients to their own devices until further help could be called about an hour later.

I cannot understand or accept the fact that those of us in a very delicate mental state can be treated so appallingly. This is 2010 – how long will it take to pull the system together to treat us in the way we deserve when so ill? Is it the funding that prevents this, is it the staff who have very little understanding of mental illness, or is it just plain neglect? It is so essential to improve these standards, as people such as myself and many others will take extreme steps to avoid a much-needed admission due to our prior experiences. Some of us could be in danger of losing our life to the illness, but the fear often outweighs the risks.

Urgent changes need to take place. All psychiatric staff should be receiving ongoing training in order to develop a better understanding of the patient's needs. They need to be educated on a variety of mental illnesses and the effects on the patient. They need to develop a more empathic approach, which in turn would give us sufferers an actual sense of comfort when admitted to hospital. Why has this not been taken in hand?

Finally, my most recent concern about perceptions of bipolar disorder in society relates to the fact that bipolar disorder appears to be becoming a rather 'fashionable' illness for many celebrities. It's almost treated like an accessory, an excuse for drug abuse, alcoholism and absurd behaviour. This doesn't benefit your normal 'lay person', who struggles with this disorder on a daily basis. The image created by celebrities only serves to add to the stigma attached to bipolar disorder.

Bipolar disorder and society: Michael Little

> I think I have been very fortunate to have family and friends who are very understanding and supportive. But on several occasions I have recognized how easily it might be different. There have been times when I could have become homeless or in great financial difficulties had my parents not been willing and able to help me. At these moments I think of others who may not have the same support.
>
> When we talk about society, we are making generalizations and mostly these are based upon our own, sometimes narrow, experiences. Despite my generally positive experiences, I would be naïve to say that all is well. Mental illness is still too often a taboo subject. Something that people would rather not speak about publicly. I often used to avoid telling people about the condition, because of what they might think about me. 'Mental' and 'depression' are still very loaded words. Words I try to avoid using. Sometimes I find myself in a conversation with someone who doesn't know about my experiences and I cringe as they joke about 'asylums' or express fear about the emotionally ill. It does happen quite often, and whilst I do not always explain my own condition, I nearly always try to put the record straight. The media probably are a lot to blame with some very exaggerated stories involving mental illness and violent crime. Let's face it – for every murder or attack by someone who was suffering mental illness, there has to be many more instigated by someone who was simply angry. But that wouldn't sell too many papers!

Bipolar disorder and society: Kate Brunwin

Kate describes the experience of being in a mental health institution in 2009.

On 17 May 2009 I was admitted as an inpatient detained under Section Three of the Mental Health Act 1983. I had concerned my family by behaving 'strangely', namely being in what I can only describe as a heightened state of consciousness, which led to delusional thinking and according behaviour. I was under the impression that I had been called to be, of all things, the Antichrist's mother and that was the driving force behind my actions. I was having hectic conversations with God and I was finding it difficult to relate this into everyday life. I stopped eating, smoked myself into oblivion and trashed my bedroom as I could not function in an orderly fashion. I was not aggressive, in fact quite the opposite. However, my mood was labelled 'labile', meaning to be prone to quick changes.

The sectioning itself was fairly harmless; as this was the second time that I had been sectioned I knew what to expect. The first time three years ago I was not really aware of what force could be used. This was partially because of my incapacity at the time, but also because of an oversight of the medical team who did not explain to me the utter seriousness of the situation. A 20-minute fight to get me into the ambulance ensued. I lost, and, completely wearied, allowed them to strap me in to the back of the ambulance, all the while seeing this through delusionary eyes, thinking they were some kind of task force who did not want the prophecy to come true.

So, this time things went fairly smoothly and I drove with my mum to the hospital. Upon arrival I was shown to my shared small room, in which the windows did not open more than 10cm even in the sweltering heat of an early summer. I was given various pieces of paperwork, but it was not until three days later that I was actually informed that I was under section, and there was me thinking that I was a voluntary patient! This was infuriating and seemed to me to show the inconsistencies involved with the bureaucracy of the system. At no point did any of the somewhat belligerent staff sit me down and attempt to understand what was going on. They seemed to be heaped under a pile of paperwork and protocol most of the time or involved in mainly reading the newspaper and watching TV at others. No one had any idea of the delusions that I was being subjected to as part of my condition simply because no one bothered to ask.

The worst aspect of being institutionalized is the heavy-handed and considerably out-dated technique of manual restraint that can be used. If the staff feel (and it is down to staff discretion) that an individual is being too labile or aggressive then they are permitted to grab that individual and twist and bend their hands and arms in such a way as to cause abject pain. This happened to me on more occasions than I deserved for a technique that should surely only be used in desperate times. I even saw it happen to one girl who rather logically refused her PRN (emergency highly sedative medication), said her piece and then calmly walked away from staff. They piled on her all three of them, large burly men, and 'escorted' her to her room as she screamed. They injected her with her medication and left her crying in pain. No follow-up measure was taken.

On various occasions I was given PRN when it had been taken off my chart and at times when I was, albeit a little erratic, not aggressive or demanding. It seems to be a way in which the staff give themselves a break from certain individuals to whom they have a duty of care.

The food was abominable. I became a vegetarian within a few weeks only to be told that there was not enough food ordered for vegetarians as it was all sorted two months in advance. There were three of us vegetarians eating two Quorn sausages one night! How this is therapeutic I will never know.

In all, my experience of being in a mental health institution sums up the neglect that the mental health system is going through. It is out-dated and in desperate need of a revamp, too many of the staff are demoralized (although certain individuals were fantastic) and uncaring, even hostile at times and there is not enough one-to-one time on the ward with the psychiatrists or psychologists. The Mental Health Act that we currently operate under in England and Wales was written in 1983, with amendments since then. It seems that it is time for a rethink.

Thankfully I recovered three months later, due to a change in medication, to having time away from work and meeting new people. I hope never to be put through such a situation again. It is all that I can hope that this will never be repeated and that my medication and living a therapeutic lifestyle will be enough to keep me safe in future.

In retrospect, this three months of my life was the best of times and the worst of times. The best because I was operating in a different world in which I was a leader and I made a lot of friends with whom I am still in contact. But also it is terrible to be locked up, to be dictated to and to be made to feel like part of a freak show. I hope that I never have to go through this again.

Bipolar disorder and society: Sandy Knox

I don't know anyone with bipolar who has been successful in keeping their life, their job and their family together. Instead, I hear of people who have lost everything to this illness. I hear of sufferers whose marriages have dissolved, whose careers have been destroyed and whose families are in tatters. People who now live reclusive lifestyles, cut off from all but a few trusted family and friends. People who are living on state benefits, with no hope of getting back to work. People who struggle and fight for appropriate medical treatment, and people who've just given up on everything.

Mental illness is still viewed with suspicion and fear, but it is a far cry from the way it used to be when sufferers were locked away, given cold baths and electroconvulsive therapy (ECT) without anaesthesia, thank God. Having said that, it is clear to those of us who suffer that very little else has changed.

Bipolar disorder is difficult to diagnose. Not least because your doctor may only see depression. After all, when you feel well or are manic, you wouldn't even consider seeing a doctor, as there would be no need, because you don't feel unwell. So the first obstacle is the diagnosis and doctors are reluctant to diagnose bipolar until they've witnessed the full spectrum of the illness which consists of both mania and depression. Consequently, it can take many months to achieve the correct diagnosis and if your doctor diagnoses depression in the first instance, as is often the case, they will prescribe antidepressants, which, taken without a mood stabilizer, can trigger 'rapid cycling'. For example, I was diagnosed with bipolar by a private psychiatrist, but it took four years to get a bipolar diagnosis from an NHS psychiatrist, thus four long, excruciatingly hard years of fighting for treatment. This scenario is not uncommon. The main reason for the four-year fight is because I rarely saw the same psychiatrist – psychiatrist retention is a huge problem within the NHS.

If bipolar disorder goes untreated, it doesn't take a genius to conclude that other aspects of one's life will be affected. Bipolar disorder is hard enough when you've been correctly diagnosed, but undiagnosed bipolar is harder still, because without that official diagnosis you will forever remain in no man's land, alone, without help, support, understanding and treatment. Could it be any worse?

As I have said, I don't know of any bipolar sufferer who is successfully living with this illness, meaning living a normal life. Many don't work, because they can't. Many, like me, have lost their jobs and are now dependent on benefits and here we have another fight on our hands. The process by which you claim benefits is much too complex when you are in the depths of depression. Completing forms which are clearly designed for physical ill health not mental ill health and phone calls to emotionless, unempathetic voices is not just hard, but almost impossible. There is help to be had, to assist you through this process, for example the Citizens Advice Bureau in the UK. But you have to ask, and asking is as hard as completing the forms yourself.

You find yourself out of work, penniless and seemingly alone. You may not be able to answer the phone or the door. You can't eat, sleep or wash. You sleep as much as you dare. You are frightened, petrified and then you receive a letter from the job centre asking you to attend a back-to-work interview. The letter floors you and if you don't attend the appointment without good reason your benefits will be stopped, usually without warning. To reinstate benefits you have to write letters and attach a letter from your doctor, complete more forms and hope for the best.

Bipolar disorder and society: Karen Paige

Accepting my diagnosis has been a journey and I'm not all the way there yet. Self-acceptance is hard, as my views are shaped by society, and society, as we know, holds negative images of people with mental illness, perpetuating prejudice and discrimination. As part of society, my views about myself having a mental illness were very negative; it was something I wasn't prepared to accept and therefore would not be able to manage. Having come to a point where I now accept my mental illness I feel at ease. While mental illness can mean unfathomable pain there have also been delicious times where the secrets and synchronicity of the universe have been revealed.

What I have not been able to do is to be open about my mental illness beyond my very immediate circle. And within that circle itself, I pretty much hide everything that I can, and only share what needs to be shared. It would be liberating to be able to speak openly, but there is such a lack of understanding, and when I've tried before on a personal level, people have got it wrong. It's hard to keep talking when you are not sure how that lack of understanding links to people's values. I have had to be open at work as I had a severe episode whilst in employment and have subsequently continued to work for that employer. I feel I would be further in my career had I not become unwell, as my lack of confidence has meant not pursuing promotions, and staying loyal to my employer, as I know they know about my health and disability. New relationships are also hard. I spent a long time concentrating all my efforts and energy on managing myself, my work and my family. It was strange adjusting my routine when routine is a big part of self-management. It has been healing to reveal what feels like big secrets: Hey, I've had ECT, oh, and another time I was sectioned. But there is love after mental illness! I look forward to the time when I can comfortably reply to the dentist when they ask about medication, not feel self-conscious when collecting my prescription from the chemist, not do everything I can to avoid telling my employer I need reasonable adjustments, not pretend to the children that I am tired, be able to tell the football coach I can't get my son there because I can't stop crying. I look forward to the day when the experiences that I have had will be recognized as a wider human consciousness bringing insight as well as pain.

Bipolar disorder and society: Tracey

The stigma of living with bipolar is getting less, partly thanks to people raising awareness, like *The Secret Life of the Manic Depressive*, a BBC documentary presented by Stephen Fry in September 2008. It seems like the 'in thing' to have it, but bipolar is a life-altering, devastating condition that can ruin your life if you let it. My bipolar does not define who I am – it is just a 'thing' that I have to live with!

In order to keep it in check, get a hobby – I make things out of papier mâché and I paint. Make sure you develop a good network of a few people you can trust. Don't share your problems with everyone – some can't cope and you may lose a few friends. Join a support organization. Go to support group meetings, take your medication regularly, take early action if your mood is going too high or too low. And LAUGH!

7 | Conclusion

CHAPTER

It was difficult for me at the start of writing this book to think about writing the conclusion as, to be honest, I wasn't sure I'd get to the end! Having bipolar and writing a book to a deadline has, to date, been the hardest task I have ever taken on, with my mood shifts dictating my working capacity. Yet here I am: I *never* give up without a fight! While it might seem unremarkable to anyone not living with mental illness, this whole project has been the most outstanding experience for me – it exceeds any other life achievement apart, of course, from having my two daughters.

As well as the actual writing process, it has been a process of learning more about bipolar disorder through thinking about my own experiences and those of the people who have kindly contributed to this book.

There are some who will say that my girls shouldn't be exposed to my depressive episodes, my endless tears, and my mental illness in general (everyone is allowed an opinion), but in seeking their opinions I have spoken honestly with my daughters, Gina and Tasha, and we have used the process of writing this book as an opportunity to discuss the subject as a family.

Gina and Tasha tell me adamantly that, because of my bipolar, they have actually become better people. They wouldn't want me any other way, they say, and always love to be around me despite everything. They recognize and admire the fact that I always wear a smile, love them to pieces, and, most importantly, that I have the ability to fight the negatives at all times. Both girls have developed into the most loving, warm, caring, fun loving and empathic individuals.

With hindsight, apart from my own experiences, I initially knew very little about this subject. I am therefore so overwhelmed by all of those who have contributed to my increased understanding – the wonderful people I have spoken to, the people I have met, the friends I have made. I cannot thank my contributors and their families enough, for giving me the opportunity to live out my dream of putting together a 'bible' of inside knowledge about bipolar disorder. Without them there would be no book.

I found each and every story incredibly interesting. Some are very sad, some are quite disturbing. I think I expected that, but I truly didn't expect to feel as astounded as I do by the fact that each person has bravely written an undeniably extremely honest and 'from the heart' account of their own personal experience. It feels, for me, as though I have already succeeded in exactly what I set out to achieve when I embarked on this project.

We all tend to voice our grief for life before bipolar disorder. Certain aspects of all of our lives have been lost along the way: marriage breakdowns, friendships broken, initial loss of custody of our children, our identity, reliability, drive and determination. We have all suffered from bucket-loads of guilt, none of which we should really carry with us, because any illness, physical or mental, is not our choice.

But for all this, I feel that if we all sat back and reflected on these difficult years, we could focus on some of the more positive aspects of our lives that have come about as a direct result of our bipolar.

Of course, here, I can only speak for myself. Yes, there has been some pretty negative material throughout this book. But had I not had bipolar disorder, I would never have met my wonderful partner Basil whom I absolutely adore. I wouldn't have gained or maintained the wonderful and loyal friendships with others that I now have. I would have continued to work ridiculous hours, under extreme pressure and, quite possibly, might not have developed the wonderful relationship I have with my daughters. We are extremely close, we talk as opposed to 'speak', we have so much fun and are all very tactile and loving towards each other.

Turning my attention back to my contributors, it appears that most of them have gained so much from their illness, as have I.

Their partners and family adore and admire their strength. Their children love and respect them, and all speak very positively about their parent. Many of these children stress that they have become better people and stronger individuals as a result of their bipolar disorder.

I now appreciate the good things in life. I take nothing for granted. I enjoy it while it's mine. I make the most out of life at every given opportunity. I can even recognize the humour that goes hand in hand with a manic episode. It is a natural process for me to reflect and laugh. What I have here, as do most of the contributors, is an appreciation of the smaller things in life, which are not always ours for the asking.

In an ideal world, perhaps most of us would choose not to have bipolar. But there is no denying the fact that it is a condition for life. We have to embrace it as part of ourselves, focus on the more positive aspects, move forward and concentrate on our future goals.

Living a life with bipolar disorder really is a case of fight or flight. I know what I would choose every time.

Further Reading

Contemporary first-person accounts on this subject include:

Behrman, A. (2002) *Electroboy: A Memoir of Mania*. New York: Random House.

Jamison, K. R. (1995) *An Unquiet Mind: A Memoir of Moods and Madness*. New York: Knopf.

Simon, L. (2002) *Detour: My Bipolar Road Trip in 4-D*. New York: Simon and Schuster.

For a practical guide to living with bipolar disorder from the perspective of the sufferer:

Kelly, M. (2005) *Bipolar and the Art of Roller-coaster Riding*. Strathbogie: Two Trees Media. (Only available in electronic format, from www.twotreesmedia.com/beatbipolar.htm.)

Knox, S. (2008) *Bi-polar on Benefits (I can't be the only one)*. London: Chipmunka Publishing.

For a critique of genetic explanations of bipolar disorder:

Joseph, J. (2006) *The Missing Gene: Psychiatry, Heredity, and the Fruitless Search for Genes*. New York: Algora.

For the perspective of a parent of children with bipolar disorder:

Earley, P. (2006) *Crazy*. New York: G.P. Putnam's Sons.

Raeburn, P. (2004) *Acquainted with the Night: A Parent's Quest to Understand Depression and Bipolar Disorder in His Children*. New York: Broadway.

Classic works on this subject include:

Goodwin, K. and Redfield Jamison, K. (1990) *Manic-Depressive Illness*. New York: Oxford University Press Inc. (The standard, very lengthy, medical reference on bipolar disorder.)

Kraepelin, E. (1921) *Manic-depressive Insanity and Paranoia*. Manchester, NH: Ayer Company. (English translation of the original German from the earlier eighth edition of Kraepelin's textbook – now outdated, but a work of major historical importance.)

Kuipers, L. and Bebbington, P. (2004) *Living with Mental Illness*. London: Souvenir Press.

Redfield Jamison, K. (1993) *Touched With Fire: Manic-Depressive Illness and the Artistic Temperament*. New York: The Free Press.

Padesky, C. and Greenberger, D. (1995) *Mind Over Mood: Cognitive Treatment Therapy Manual for Clients*. London: Guilford Press.

Townsend, M. (2007) *The Father I Had*. London: Bantam Press.

An excellent novel for children about a mother with bipolar disorder is:

Wilson, J. (2000) *The Illustrated Mum*. London: Corgi Yearling.

Various publications are available from MDF The Bipolar Organization (www.mdf.org.uk), including:

Copeland, M. and McKay, M. (2003) *The Depression Workbook: A Guide for Living with Manic Depression*. Oakland, CA: New Harbinger Publications.

Faulkner, A. (1997) *Knowing Our Own Minds: A Survey of How People in Emotional Distress Take Control of Their Lives*. London: Mental Health Foundation.

Leaflets, such as the following, are also available from MDF The Bipolar Organization. (Many carers would highly recommend these leaflets, as they have found them to be very helpful and easy to read.)

Why Did My World Have to Change?
Manic Depression Bipolar Disorder.
Drug Treatment of Manic Depression.
Planning Ahead.
Information for Family and Friends.
The Enduring Power of Attorney.
Bipolar Disorder in Children and Young People.
Employers Guide to Manic Depression and Employment.

Useful Organizations

UK organizations

Saneline

www.sane.org.uk

Tel: 08457 678000 (1pm–11pm daily)

SANE aims to raise awareness of and support people with mental illness and their families, and undertakes research into the causes of mental iillness.

MDF The Bipolar Organization

www.mdf.org.uk

Tel: 08456 340 540

MDF The Bipolar Organization aims to enable people affected by bipolar to take control of their lives.

ChildLine

www.childline.org.uk/Pages/Home.aspx

Tel: 0800 1111 (24 hours)

ChildLine is a counselling service for children and young people.

Samaritans

www.samaritans.org/

Tel: 08457 909090

Samaritans provides confidential non-judgemental emotional support 24 hours a day for people who are experiencing feelings of distress or despair.

Carers UK

www.carersuk.org/Home

Tel: 020 7490 8818

Carers UK supports carers and campaigns for better recognition of carers.

Young Carers Initiative

www.youngcarer.com/showPage.php?file=index.htm

Tel: 01962 711 511

The Young Carers Initiative works nationally to promote good practice for young carers and their families.

The Princess Royal Trust for Carers

www.carers.org

Tel: 020 7480 7788

The Princess Royal Trust for Carers is the largest provider of comprehensive carers support services in the UK.

Bipolar Carers Trust

Tel: 01873 856314 or 07798 6662477

US organizations

American Mental Health Foundation

http://americanmentalhealthfoundation.org/amhf.php?id=6

Tel: 1 212 737 9027 or 1 212 414 2275 ext 16

The American Mental Health Foundation (AMHF) is a research organization dedicated to the welfare of people suffering from emotional problems.

Clifford Beers Foundation

www.cliffordbeersfoundation.co.uk

The Clifford Beers Foundation is a world wide organization that works to promote mental health and prevent mental disorders through dissemination of knowledge, training partnerships and consultation.

Depression and Bipolar Support Alliance (DBSA)

www.dbsalliance.org

Tel: 800 826 3632 (Toll free)

The Depression and Bipolar Support Alliance aims to provide hope, help and support to improve the lives of people living with depression or bipolar disorder by offering peer-based, recovery-oriented, empowering services and resources.

Family and Home Network

www.FamilyandHome.org
Email: fahn@familyandhome.org
The Family and Home Network is a support network that offers advice to help families to spend generous amounts of time together by focusing on children's need for warm, nurturing relationships with their parents.

Mental Health America

www.mentalhealthamerica.net
Tel: 800 969 6642 (Toll free)
Mental Health America is a community-based network dedicated to helping all Americans live mentally healthier lives.

National Alliance on Mental Illness

www.nami.org
Tel: 1 800 950 6264
The National Alliance on Mental Illness provides easy-to-understand information about mental illnesses, mental health care, diagnosis, treatment and recovery, as well as links to programmes, services and support groups for people whose lives have been affected by mental illness.

New Jersey Parents' Caucus

www.newjerseyparentscaucus.org
Tel: 973 989 8866
The New Jersey Parents' Caucus is a coalition of families whose mission is to ensure that every family who has children with special emotional and behavioral needs is given an opportunity to play a strong and active role in the development and delivery of effective and timely services for their children.

Appendix: List of Stories

Index